"In this book Cameron Cole provides us with a framework for the spiritual practice of cultivating a heavenly imagination. When we are confronted with weariness and the sting of death, heaven breaks into our present reality. Through pain, we can access a deeper joy even now as we wait for that restoration that we will one day know in full. This is a courageous and vulnerable encouragement and offers us a way of wisdom through difficulty."

Sandra McCracken, singer-songwriter

"Heavenward drew me in because of Cameron Cole's story. Who better to guide us through a studied, biblical understanding of eternity and how it affects our two o'clock on a Monday than one who has lost a child? I'm grateful for these sage words and the story behind them."

Sara Hagerty, author, *Every Bitter Thing Is Sweet* and *Adore*

"Cameron Cole invites readers to the heavenward life, and this book equips them for a journey of eschatological sanctification. He shows how looking upward in Christ helps humanize us and grants us resilient hope for times both good and bad. He writes as a fellow pilgrim of the transforming vision that he's seen and longs to share."

Michael Allen, John Dyer Trimble Professor of Systematic Theology and Academic Dean, Reformed Theological Seminary, Orlando

" 'The end defines the story.' These profound words capture the essence of Cameron Cole's life-giving wisdom and insight in *Heavenward*. It will help shed the earthly minded scales from your eyes and lift your gaze to see not only the promises of your future heavenly home but also the beautiful reality that heaven has already come to us through our union with Jesus. May it encourage your heart with the truth that the hope of tomorrow directly infuses hope into the realities of today."

Sarah Walton, coauthor, *He Gives More Grace*; *Hope When It Hurts*; and *Together Through the Storms*

Heavenward

Heavenward

How Eternity Can Change Your Life on Earth

Cameron Cole

WHEATON, ILLINOIS

Library of Congress Cataloging-in-Publication Data

Names: Cameron, Cole, 1979– author.
Title: Heavenward : how eternity can change your life on earth / Cole Cameron.
Description: Wheaton, Illinois : Crossway, 2024. | Includes bibliographical references and index.
Identifiers: LCCN 2023024204 (print) | LCCN 2023024205 (ebook) | ISBN 9781433590238 (trade paperback) | ISBN 9781433590245 (pdf) | ISBN 9781433590269 (epub) Subjects: LCSH: Bible. Epistles of Paul—Theology. | God (Christianity)—Eternity. | Church history. | Heaven—Biblical teaching.
Classification: LCC BS2655.H34 C36 2024 (print) | LCC BS2655.H34 (ebook) | DDC 236/.24—dc23/eng/20231002
LC record available at https://lccn.loc.gov/2023024204
LC ebook record available at https://lccn.loc.gov/2023024205

Crossway is a publishing ministry of Good News Publishers.

VP   33   32   31   30   29   28   27   26   25   24
15   14   13   12   11   10   9   8   7   6   5   4   3   2   1

To my spectacular, beautiful, and precious daughter,
Mary Matthews
You are a special gift from heaven above.
You are and always have been a perpetual joy to your
mother and me and to everyone who knows you.
I give God daily thanks for who you are.

Contents

Introduction

ON THE DAY MY OLDEST CHILD DIED, I received a message from a friend that simply read, "How long, O Lord? How long?" This message encapsulates so much of the Christian life. We suffer in the fallen world. We wait for the return of Christ. We aim to move fruitfully toward glory.

In the Christian life, all things begin, point to, and end in eternity. For most of my life, I did not live with this awareness, but that changed radically one Veterans Day.

On November 11, 2013, my perspective shifted *heavenward*. On that day, my precious, vibrant, curly-haired, little boy Cam went to live with God in heaven above. On November 10, 2013, my three-year-old Cam professed faith in Christ after asking if we could "get in the car" to go see Jesus. He expressed a desire to visit Christ in heaven above. The next day, my perfectly healthy Cam shockingly and unexpectedly entered God's eternal glory. He went to sleep in our home; he woke up above in the arms of Jesus.

Amidst the sorrow and grief of my child's death, something radically new happened in my daily mindset. Heaven became an almost ever-present part of my perspective. This transformation made sense: this is where my firstborn child now lived.

The Eternal Problem

The primary problem in the spiritual lives of modern Christians is *eschatological* in nature. *Eschatology* is a fancy theological word for matters related to heaven and the end times. This book addresses that problem.

With each passing second, every person's life is moving toward eternity. However, most Christians live with very little awareness of their eternal trajectory. Other Christians, as a product of life circumstances such as suffering, death, or a terminal diagnosis, do have an awareness of heaven. Still, they have very little knowledge or structure to offer them meaningful, life-giving direction as they move toward glory.

Consequently, to put it in sophisticated, academic language, one could describe the spiritual lives of many Christians as blah or meh. Perhaps, you can identify with this feeling. Your relationship with Christ lacks the deep joy and abundant life that Jesus offers. You do not experience the soaring hope and steadfast perseverance described in the New Testament. Your service to Christ feels routine and obligatory and does not contain transcendent inspiration or bold resolve.

Of course, God does not promise constant "highs" in the Christian life, and yet you can reasonably expect more than a nondescript relationship with Jesus. God's grace to us in Jesus contains too much richness for such flatness.

A spiritual perspective quietly pervading the modern church involves what the apostle Paul referred to as "earthly mindedness" (see Phil. 3:19). A present-day term for earthly mindedness is YOLO:

"You only live once." In other words, modern Christians often live as if this life is it. There's no heaven beyond. As a result, there's little to no eternal hope, joy, or purpose in the spirituality of many Christians.

Consequently, people chase fleeting pleasures of this life, which do not satisfy their souls. They freak out when difficulties and trials come their way. They conceive of their purpose and mission for Christ in a manner that elicits little inspiration or boldness.

You may be reading this and thinking, "My heart and mind are anywhere but in this life." For you, a death, a diagnosis, or a general sense of disenchantment with this world has turned your soul away from the earth. In a general, undirected way, your consciousness has shifted toward eternity. Still, you do not know exactly where to go with these feelings and longings.

Game-changing transformation occurs when we set our hearts and minds "on things above," as Paul exhorted believers to do (Col. 3:1–2). Life-altering change can happen when we live like citizens of heaven, as Paul characterized believers (see Phil. 3:20). Your Christian life can be turned upside-down when you start to live *heavenward*. Christ calls us there, and the apostle Paul gives us direction.

A *heavenward* life means that heaven serves as the backdrop of your everyday consciousness. Heaven is a frequent object of your longings and desires. In a *heavenward* life, eternity organically and instinctively informs and drives the everyday matters of your life.

I can tell you from personal experience that you will discover and enjoy great spiritual riches in a *heavenward* life.

My Friend, the Apostle Paul

A heavenward mindset changed my life after my son died. As the sorrow of grief subsided, *heavenwardness* provided richer fellowship with Jesus. I had more perspective and more hope. I had more comfort and more patience. I had more focus in ministry, prayer, and evangelism. Life set in relation to heaven felt more hopeful, joyful, and purposeful. Though I was suffering deeply from the loss of my son, God was blessing my inner life in a unique way, like I had never before experienced.

However, I do not know if I would have sustained this heavenward life after the season of grief if I had not met a significant companion on the heavenly journey.

During that year after Cam died, I was thinking about heaven so much that I started to feel weird. I would forget to pay a bill and conclude, "That twenty-five-dollar late fee won't matter in heaven." I'd miss a college reunion and figure, "I'll see those friends in glory." *Surely nobody was thinking in such an abnormal way.*

Meanwhile, I began reading the letters of the apostle Paul in my devotional life. As I read these New Testament books, I noticed heaven popping up all over the place! I used a golden highlighter (like the heavenly streets of gold) to mark every reference to heaven and eternity in Paul's letters. My Bible was covered with yellow highlights in the Pauline epistles.

When he talks about suffering, he mentions the resurrection of the body or being at home with God. When he considers morality and ethics, the heavenly realities of the kingdom of God appear. When Paul thinks about serving God, seeing Christ on his judgment seat motivates him.

Heaven pervaded the consciousness and life of the apostle Paul. In one sense, he lived as a person whose life was constantly moving toward glory. In another sense, Paul lived as if he were already there.

I had found a friend, someone who had thought about heaven in an even more intense, constant, and peculiar manner than I had.

What I discovered is that my life had been moving heavenward since the day of my conversion as a young person. God used the fact that my child lived in glory to awaken me to the present heavenly realities of my salvation. Paul did have circumstances that probably aided his heavenly awakening. He characterized his life as "*often* near death" (2 Cor. 11:23). In his letter to the Philippians, one gets the impression that Paul was not sure if his imprisonment would end in death or deliverance (Phil. 1:18–26). In 2 Corinthians, he mentions being beaten nearly to death five times and adrift at sea for a full day and a full night after a shipwreck (2 Cor. 11:25).

However, the realities brought about through Jesus's life, death, resurrection, and ascension (known as the Christ Event) more likely drove and sustained Paul's heavenward life.

Paul viewed the Christ Event as the arrival of heaven on earth. The Christ Event signified the beginning of the age to come, a new heavenly age, which Jews had anticipated for centuries. Paul's letters clearly assert that the conversion of believers means that they are instantly transferred into the kingdom of heaven, and they live as citizens of that heavenly realm where Christ reigns in his glory.

As I continued to study heaven, I found other heavenward friends along the way in the writings and music of church history. The early church fathers, Christian mystics, Puritan theologians, British poets, slaves of the American South, and others all became heavenward companions. From these sources, I found other people who were consumed with heaven to various degrees.

In this season, my life changed radically. I want this change for you too.

When you understand the implications of the coming of Christ and the fullness of your salvation, heaven naturally starts to sink deeper and deeper into your heart and mind. You start to realize that, in the spiritual realm, you live with a foot in heaven and a toe on earth. The more eternity sinks into your soul, the more your life, actions, and longings move in a heavenward direction.

When you realize that God has blessed you in Christ with "all the spiritual blessings in the heavenly places," greater joy enters your relationship with Jesus. When you digest how eternally blissful your life in heaven will be, the more you can persevere in the trials and sufferings of this life. When you think about offering your life as a worshipful gift before the judgment seat of Christ, the more inspiring and convicted your purpose in life becomes.

The apostle Paul's theology of heaven offers promise and hope in these various areas. All of these eternal benefits and blessings are on offer to you right now in the gospel.

The Map of the Journey Ahead

As we depend on God's grace together, *Heavenward* will be a journey toward a heart, mind, and life more anchored in glory and more filled with joy, hope, and purpose.

Section 1, "The Beginning of the Heavenward Journey," features a short, basic overview of the components of heaven, largely drawn from Paul's theology. It also defines what I mean by a "heavenward life."

Section 2 looks at "Why Paul Was So Heavenward (And You Can Be Too!)." We will look at five different factors in Paul's life and theology that influenced his heavenwardness. In the process, we will find that these factors in Paul's life are true of your life and the lives of all Christians.

Finally, in section 3, we will discuss and enjoy "The Fruit of a Heavenward Life." We will explore five benefits and promises that flow out of Paul's heavenward mentality. In doing so, we will see the transformative and hopeful power of living with a heavenward trajectory.

An important note: section 2 contains much information about the present realities and implications of heaven. If you are reading this book primarily because of a curiosity about heaven, you will likely find these chapters fascinating. If you are reading this book during a season of deep grief and sorrow and primarily looking for encouragement, you could get bogged down in the teaching portions. I encourage you to stick with the more informational passages because these portions will help you and ground you as they provide essential foundations for the hope of heaven now and for the rest of your life. I would also say that you will find lots of encouragement at the ends of these chapters in the "Your Heavenward Journey" segments, and then in section 3 which covers the fruit of a heavenward life.

For Whom This Book Is Written

This book is written for two groups of people. First, it is written for the person who is aware that his or her life is moving heavenward. If you see yourself here, perhaps you have lost a loved one and, as a result, heaven is filling your heart and mind. You are thinking constantly about your loved one and his or her life above. Or maybe you're becoming more aware of your mortality as a result of a terminal diagnosis or natural aging. It could be that you've grown weary of this broken world and find yourself saying, "Come, Lord Jesus," as if it's the refrain of your life. Regardless of the reason, if your life is moving heavenward, this book will help you channel that heavenly trajectory in a manner that yields redemption, hope, joy, and meaning.

Second, this book is for the person who is not fully aware that his or her life is moving heavenward. If that's you, your spiritual life has become stale and flat, and you're longing for something more in your faith. However, you have not identified that God is shifting your heart, mind, and actions toward eternity. The heavenly trajectory on which the Lord is sending you promises to rekindle a richness and joy that you have not tasted in a long time or ever. Paul and other heavenward friends can serve as your guide in the same way they were for me in my inspiring journey.

Regardless of your situation, this is an invitation to join the "upward call" to which Paul directs believers (Phil. 3:14). This is an invitation to a *heavenward* life.

THE BEGINNING OF THE HEAVENWARD JOURNEY

1

Paul and Heaven

THE AIM OF THIS BOOK is to see the Lord transform people's lives by gaining a heavenward mindset. The first step in this journey involves learning or reviewing some of the basic structures and components related to heaven, particularly those found in Paul's letters and theology. After all, it is pretty challenging to meditate on and long for heaven if you are not clear on what eternity entails.

People often have bits and pieces of knowledge about heaven but are not necessarily sure how they all fit together. This chapter, "Paul and Heaven," will help connect the dots for you by presenting a progression that will underlie the entire book: heaven, heavenly mindedness, and heavenward.

Heaven involves the details and knowledge about God's plans for eternity and about the believer's life with Jesus after death. (We will divide heaven into two sections: future heaven and present heaven.)

Heavenly mindedness refers to an intentional spiritual discipline whereby we deliberately meditate on heaven and the glory of God there.

Heavenward describes a work of God in your life in which heaven becomes an organic part of your daily perspective and the object of your life's direction. A *heavenward* life flows out of a knowledge of heaven, heavenly minded prayer and meditation, and the work of the Holy Spirit in your heart.

With that being said, let's start the journey with these rich, heavenly truths from Paul's theology. This chapter will be a little more on the educational side compared to the others, but it provides important foundations for the adventure ahead.

Future Heaven

When people think about heaven, usually they conceive first of what happens to us after we die. They often think about the realities that flow from Christ's second coming. You may know many of the aspects of *future heaven* but are not quite sure how they all fit together. I have divided future heaven into three intervals.

The Intermediate State

You may never have heard the term *intermediate state*, but it's probably what you are thinking about when you hear the word *heaven*. When people die in Christ before the second coming of Christ, they enter the intermediate state. Your deceased loved ones in the Lord currently dwell in the intermediate state.

In the intermediate state, believers are delivered from pain, sin, and evil (Rom. 8:18–23; 2 Cor. 5:17; Rev. 21:1–4). They will never suffer, sin, or experience the effects of the fall again. Believers gain a vision of God in his full glory and enjoy perfect union with Christ. They live in perpetual joy.

Paul tells us that, after death, we are away from our perishable, earthly bodies but do not yet have our glorified bodies, which we gain at the second coming of Christ (2 Cor. 5:8). Therefore, we are not certain about the bodily state in which we exist in the intermediate state. Nevertheless, we are perfectly happy and experience no suffering ever again.

The Second Coming of Christ

The second coming of Christ designates the end of the "present evil age" (Gal. 1:4), the time period from the fall to the second coming where sin has broken and damaged this world. A number of significant end-times events occur during or right around the time of the second coming. The order of them is not perfectly clear, so think of these more as events connected to the second coming and worry less about the sequence in which they occur.

At the second coming, Christ appears to all people. Around the time of his appearing, a *rapture* occurs, where believers on earth rise up into heaven to be with Christ and the saints for Christ's return (1 Thess. 4:16–17). People debate how soon before Christ's return believers rise into the heavens and for how long they dwell there before coming to the earth. Regardless, Paul does suggest a rising of believers into the heavens with Christ in some form (1 Thess. 4:16–17).

The *resurrection of the dead* occurs at the second coming. This event involves all people—believers and nonbelievers—gaining a new body (Acts 24:15). Believers gain a perfected, imperishable body that will never experience sickness, wounds, breaks, or pain ever again (1 Cor. 15:35–54). Think about how incredible it will be never to feel physical pain again!

After the rapture and the resurrection of the body, a *final judgment* of all humanity will occur. I believe that a separate judgment occurs for believers and nonbelievers. Christ will judge eternally those who have rejected the gospel and tried to justify themselves through works (Rom. 2:16; 2 Thess. 1:8–10). Nonbelievers are judged according to their works, rather than according to the righteousness of Jesus, which comes by grace for those who have received his salvation. They will spend eternity apart from God.

A judgment also occurs for believers before the *judgment seat of Christ*. This judgment does not determine final salvation; after all, believers have already entered heaven and dwelled there prior to sitting before the judgment seat of Christ. Here, believers give an account of their lives before Jesus and receive rewards for works of faithfulness done for the glory of Christ (Rom. 14:10–12). We do not know the nature of the rewards. We do not believe any punishment is involved, since Christ received punishment for our sins on the cross. At the same time, Paul does suggest that a loss of rewards (or better said, missed opportunity to gain them) occurs if we do not invest our lives for the glory of God (1 Cor. 3:10–15; 2 Cor. 5:10).

The New Heavens and the New Earth

After Christ returns, heaven and earth will merge. Through the final judgment, God will banish all evil from the earth and fully restore creation (Rom. 8:19–23). The Lord will dwell with his people on the earth. In the new heavens and new earth, believers will enjoy a physical existence, including food, drink, affection, sounds, and sights. The new heavens and new earth will literally be heaven on earth!

Present Heaven

Perhaps the most significant factor in Paul's heavenward mindset involves the current presence of heaven on earth as a result of the life, death, and resurrection of Jesus.[1] Let me say that again because it sounds confusing and fantastic: heaven has partially come to earth as a product of the Christ Event.[2]

In a topic that we will explore more in chapter 3, the end-times event that Jews longed for was called "the day of the Lord." In the same way that Christians wait for the second coming of Christ, Jews anticipated the day. On the day of the Lord, God himself would come to the earth in his full glory. Upon his coming he would judge the world and pour out his Holy Spirit. In addition, they expected a resurrection of the dead to occur. Best of all, after the events of the day of the Lord, a restoration of the world would occur and heaven would dwell on earth. They referred to this merging of heaven and earth as "the age to come."

When Paul saw Jesus on the road to Damascus and realized that Christ was, in fact, divine, he began to connect the dots. Christ being God meant that the Lord had come to the earth via the incarnation. When Jesus rose from the dead, Paul interpreted that as a resurrection of the dead, as was expected on the day. When Pentecost occurred, Paul viewed the event as the anticipated pouring out of the Holy Spirit. When God poured out his wrath on Jesus on the cross, a divine judgment occurred. With all of these dots connecting to the signs of the day of the Lord, Paul made

1 This spiritual reality constitutes one of the most important truths to know in the heavenward journey, so an entire chapter (chap. 3) is dedicated to it later. Consequently, I will speak briefly here.
2 Again, "Christ Event" refers to the life, death, resurrection, and ascension of Jesus.

the declaration, "Now is the favorable time; behold, now is the day of salvation" (2 Cor. 6:2).

Eureka! The day of the Lord is here—in a partial sense. As a result of the day having occurred, the age to come is now upon us. Heaven has come to the earth. We live in the new heavenly age.

This assertion may sound confusing or unbelievable to you, given the pain, darkness, and brokenness in the world. Paul does not say that the present evil age has ended. He does declare, though, that the new heavenly age has arrived through the Christ Event. It just happens to overlap with the present evil age until the second coming of Christ.

Paul uses different terminology to describe the presence of heaven on earth, such as the new creation, the kingdom of God, the Spirit, and the light. Though each image emphasizes different aspects of the age to come, they all fundamentally refer to the current presence of heaven on earth.

As you move heavenward, you must expand your conceptualization of heaven. Heaven does not just have future implications; heaven has past and present implications as well. God certainly moves your life toward glory. At the same time, heaven came—past tense—to the earth when Christ entered this realm. As a result, heaven is here and now for Christians.

As we will explore in chapter 4, heaven is the place you presently dwell. In your conversion, Christ transferred you there. Very few spiritual truths will lead you heavenward more than this one. This glorious reality changes everything.

Heavenly Mindedness

Once we understand the nature of heaven, both present and future, we are ready for the next movement in the journey. The next step involves heavenly mindedness, an intentional practice whereby we deliberately meditate on and long for heaven.

When my son died, I naturally began to think about heaven constantly. My beloved child, whom I long to be with, now lived there. My mind and heart understandably moved in an upward direction. Heavenly mindedness naturally occurred in my life. You may be able to relate to this experience in your own life. This mindset started out of my own personal experience, but Paul calls for heavenly mindedness in all believers.

Heavenly mindedness is, in fact, an exhortation of Scripture. In Colossians, Paul encourages heavenly mindedness as a practice in the Christian life:

> If then you have been raised with Christ, *seek the things that are above,* where Christ is, seated at the right hand of God. *Set your minds on things that are above*, not on things that are on earth. (Col. 3:1–2)

Without getting too academic, there are two grammatical features to notice in those verses. First, Paul calls us to set our hearts and minds on "things above" in the *imperative voice* and the *present tense*. Here's why this is important. First, the imperative voice in the Bible reflects a command of God to believers. To set our hearts and minds on heaven is less of a suggestion and more of a directive. While relying on the Holy Spirit, the Lord directs us to meditate on and long for the realities of heaven. Second, the present tense in Greek represents continuous action, not a one-time event. The Lord commands us to think about eternity as a daily habit. Heavenly mindedness serves as a deliberate, ongoing spiritual practice.

In Colossians 3, Paul also portrays heavenly mindedness as both an intellectual and an emotional exercise. In Colossians 3:2 Paul writes, "Set your minds on things that are above," emphasizing the intellectual aspect of heavenly mindedness. He reinforces this intellectual practice in 2 Corinthians, when he writes, "We look not to the things that are seen but to the things that are unseen. For the things that are seen are transient, but the things that are unseen are eternal" (2 Cor. 4:18). We turn our minds toward eternal truths and realities.

For me, this meditation began with my thinking about what my son's life looked like in eternity. I can specifically remember considering how the luminescence of Christ's glory may glow off of Cam's white locks. I would envision him sitting in Christ's lap and engulfed by Jesus's embrace.

As time went on, and as I received guidance in Paul's letters, I started to base my thinking about heaven on the images of Scripture, particularly those provided in Revelation. I would consider Christ seated on his throne with heavenly creatures glorifying him. I would think about the city of God with its streets of gold and dazzling gems adorning it. I would envision the beauty and majesty of the restored earth. *What may the waters and mountains and grassy fields of the new earth look like?*

Howard Thurman wrote that the heavenly mindedness of American slaves (as seen in slave spirituals) contained both an objective and a personal quality. He wrote, "Heaven was specific! An orderly series of events was thought to take place. . . . A crown, a personal crown is given. . . . There are mansions. . . . There are slippers."[3] As referenced in the Bible, they thought

3   Howard Thurman, *The Negro Spiritual Speaks of Life and Death* (Richmond, IN: Friends United Press, 1975), 53.

about the crown and the home of heaven. But it wasn't just *a* crown or *a* home; it was *their* crown and *their* home. Scriptural truths provided the grounds of their heavenly mindedness, but the personal relevance of these realities fueled their heavenly mindset.

Paul's portrayal of heavenly mindedness comprised more than just an intellectual exercise. When he encouraged believers to seek things above, his exhortation included the emotions and desires of the heart. One could characterize this aspect of heavenly mindedness as heavenly longing. In Romans 8:23 Paul writes that "not only the creation, but we ourselves . . . *groan inwardly* as we wait eagerly for the adoption as sons, the redemption of our bodies." You can almost feel the yearning for glory, the yearning for deliverance, the yearning to see the glory of God emanating from the core of Paul's soul with the words "groan inwardly."

Don't you know this groaning? I know I sure do. I groan to be delivered from the pains of this world. To be delivered from sin and sorrow and fear. To be delivered from heartburn and pulled muscles and a bad back. For the world to be delivered from war and racism and poverty. For my friends to be delivered from lupus and cancer and addiction and diabetes.

And I long to see Jesus in all of his glory! I long to feel the deep, perpetual joy of unfettered union with God. I long to praise and adore him at his very feet, not as a matter of faith but as a natural response to seeing his majesty.

And I long to see my little boy and to hold him again and to run my hands through his soft hair and to kiss his ruddy full cheeks and to play with him, with the light of Christ illuminating all of our interactions.

Now this, my friends, is the fuller picture of heavenly mindedness. In the mind, we imagine and meditate, considering images and realities that come out of Scripture. And with the heart we long and desire in a manner that elevates our whole self onto an eternal plain.

Heavenly mindedness, though, is not something we manufacture by effort. Yes, we certainly use intentionality and discipline, as we do with any spiritual practice. We grow in our biblical knowledge of heaven so that truth is the "material" of our meditations. Simultaneously, we rely on the Holy Spirit to grow us in heavenly mindedness.

The Christian mystic Teresa of Ávila wrote *The Interior Castle*, a book about her spiritual journey into Christ's heavenly glory through prayer. In an extended metaphor Teresa went room by room in a spiritual castle, closer and closer to Christ. As she portrayed images from her own heavenly mindedness, Teresa offered this admonition: "But we cannot enter by any efforts of our own, His Majesty must put us right into the centre of our soul, and must enter there Himself, in order that He may the better show us His wonders."[4]

In the following Puritan prayer, the speaker models both the practice of heavenly mindedness and the necessary reliance on Christ for an eternal mindset:

In needful transactions let my affection be in heaven,
and my love soar upwards in flames of fire,
my gaze fixed on unseen things,
my eyes open to the emptiness, fragility,

---

4 Teresa of Ávila, *The Interior Castle* (New York: Image, 2013), 88.

mockery of earth and its vanities.
May I view all things in the mirror of eternity,
waiting for the coming of my Lord, listening for the last
    trumpet call,
hastening unto the new heaven and earth.[5]

Like the Puritan, may we ask the Lord to move our affections, love, and gaze toward God in heaven. May we recognize the emptiness of the world. May we listen and look, await and hasten Christ's coming. May we practice heavenly mindedness by the grace and power of the Holy Spirit.

Your Heavenward Journey

As you can see, your heavenly journey begins in the mind, emotions, and spirit. As we intellectually grow in biblical knowledge about heaven, we meditate on these eternal realities. As we mature spiritually our longings and desires point more and more to their satisfaction in Christ and in his heavenly kingdom. And as we move heavenward, we observe his upward movement in our lives while also trusting in the Spirit to elevate us.

One must start with intellectual knowledge about heaven. Nevertheless, at times people can focus on facts about heaven in a way in which they lose sight of the personal nature of glory. Before my son died I knew a fair amount about heaven. What made heaven so transformative after his death was that it became so deeply personal. The knowledge did far more than fulfill intellectual curiosity; it told me about my son's new home

5   Arthur G. Bennett, *The Valley of Vision: A Collection of Puritan Prayers and Devotions* (Edinburgh: Banner of Truth, 1986).

and about the place where we will spend eternity together when we reunite.

The heavenward shift involves the transformation of the whole person. As the mind and heart shift toward eternity, so will our feet. So will our lives such that we live as citizens of heaven, beings of the new creation.

Our next chapter will paint a clearer picture of what this heavenward transformation looks like in real life.

2

Heavenward

I LOVE NOTHING MORE than the Monday after Thanksgiving. Christmas season has arrived. Lights are up, stores decorated, eggnog served, and Christmas music plays constantly.

Something is special about the Christmas season. It fills your life. You still pay bills, go to work, and take out the garbage, but the holiday pervades your consciousness.

Christmas influences your actions too. The movies you watch, the gifts you buy, the candy canes you suck, the evergreen you smell, and the eggnog you sip—although you might engage in any of these pleasures on December 4, 14, or 24, they all point to December 25. You might be washing dishes, but you smell the cinnamon candle. You might be at the office, but you're drinking Starbucks Christmas Blend. You might be driving to work, but you're listening to Christmas carols in the car.

You see, think, hear, taste, and smell Christmas nearly all the time. That's Christmas season.

For Paul, you could describe his life after conversion as "heaven season." Heaven pervaded his perspective. He still made tents, took trips, ate meals, and cleaned his house, but based on the content of his epistles, we see that heaven filled his consciousness and drove his life. Paul related just about any matter in life to the present and future realities of heaven. Heaven informed his views about singleness, morality, death, evangelism, suffering, work, conflicts, sexuality, friendships, and other topics. The apostle possessed such an intense heaven consciousness in his mind because heavenly realities, brought about by the Christ Event, constitute the context of Christian existence.

Life in heaven is our present and our future. It is the backdrop and the grounds of the Christian life, now and forever.

In his letters, we can identify information about the events and details of eternity. We can also see Paul encouraging Christians to pursue a deliberate spiritual discipline of thinking about heavenly realities, which we can aptly refer to as "heavenly mindedness."

Still, we observe a next level in Paul where we see heaven functioning organically as the natural fuel, mindset, and climate of his life. Heaven seeped into his being such that he almost subconsciously lived with it influencing his thoughts, desires, and actions. I refer to this as the heavenward life.

This chapter explores the nature and characteristics of Paul's heavenwardness so that we will have a clearer picture of what it looks like for God to transform us in a way that is similar to what Paul modeled and which I have experienced. Christmas season brings joy and excitement for a month each year. The hope and presence of heaven can bring joy, hope, and purpose to all parts of our daily lives.

Life's Game Clock

When a person plays college football, there's a constant awareness of two clocks in the stadium, particularly in a close game. First, there is the play clock. After a play ends, the offense has forty seconds to snap the ball for the next play. If the clock hits zero and the team has not snapped the ball, it receives a five-yard penalty. Then there is the game clock. In the final quarter of the game, which lasts fifteen minutes, if the clock strikes zero and your team has fewer points than the other team, you lose the game. Whether we are talking about the play clock or the game clock, everyone on the field and in the stadium knows the endpoint: zero seconds. Throughout the game, everyone's eyes and heads constantly turn to maintain an awareness of how close the situation is to the endpoint.

Paul lived with a similar awareness of an endpoint. He used different terminology in different places, but for him, the second coming of Christ constituted the clear endpoint of life. In his first letter to the church in Corinth, the apostle gave thanks for the grace that God had supplied to the Corinthians in Christ, which served to sustain them "to the end, guiltless in the day of our Lord Jesus Christ" (1 Cor. 1:8). In that same letter, when giving instructions for the church to observe the sacrament of the Lord's Supper, he commanded believers to practice it "until he comes" (1 Cor. 11:26). In Philippians, Paul wrote about his desire, motivation, and expectation pointing toward experiencing "the resurrection of the dead," which will occur at the second coming (Phil. 3:11).

Because Paul had a clear endpoint, a narrative existed in his life. He had an awareness of where everything was heading. In the same way that a quarterback and a coach constantly have their head on a swivel, looking at the play clock and the game clock, Paul's mind was on a swivel, looking toward Christ's return. Because he knew that the end of the story is eternal life with Christ, he lived under a heavenly narrative.

In his first letter to the Thessalonians, Paul described the spiritual history of believers. He wrote to them, "You turned to God from idols to serve the living and true God, and to wait for his Son from heaven, whom he raised from the dead, Jesus who delivers us from the wrath to come" (1 Thess. 1:9–10). This short verse tells the whole spiritual history of a Christian's salvation and life. We turned from worshiping false gods to serving the true, living God. We were destined for judgment, but now we are heavenbound. Meanwhile, as we love, serve, and worship God, we wait for his second coming. The end defines the story.

What if you had no sense of where both your life and human history were headed? What if the afterlife were some amorphous, undefined mystery? If you have no end, you have no story. If you have no story, you have no ultimate sense of stability and comfort in life.

Have you ever watched a dramatic, suspenseful movie for the first time, not knowing how the story would end? The experience produces anxiety and inner turmoil. However, if you go back and watch the film a second or third time, you feel calmer with each viewing. The conflicts and twists in the plot become less unsettling because you know the final resolution.

Like Paul, we have a narrative. We know where the world is headed and where our lives end, and it's a happy ending. (The happiest, in fact.) Stories with happy endings give us comfort, hope, joy, and direction. These blessings of heavenwardness brought about through a real heavenly narrative belong to us through Christ.

There's a next step in the heavenward journey, though, when not only the head but also the heart lives on the heavenly swivel; the heart continually turns toward glory. In God's spiritual eco-system, what starts in the head begins to flow to the heart, the emotions, and the desires.

Howard Thurman, in writing about the salient theme of heaven in American slave spirituals, characterized life as "pilgrimage."[1] Because slaves in the American South had little to no expectation of happiness in this life at all, their hopes turned toward glory. As a result, they sang about heaven constantly in their songs. Heavenward longings pervaded their music.

One classic spiritual contains the refrain, "I'm-a travelin' to the grave" over and over. Another song calls for fellow slaves to "cheer the weary traveler, along the heavenly way." As they sang the other lyrics, they echoed these heavenly refrains over and over again. They lived with such vivid clarity and acute awareness of their heavenly destination and, consequently, of the temporality of this life. As a result, the framework of their lives was a hard, painful journey toward relief and exuberance in heaven. They took a step closer to the promised land with each day that passed.

The heavenward life observed in the American slave spirituals surpassed intellectual awareness. Their heavenwardness involved an emotional longing, almost a guttural moan from deep in their soul. Certainly, this perspective started in the mind, but one can see that

1   Howard Thurman, *The Negro Spiritual Speaks of Life and Death* (Richmond, IN: Friends United Press, 1975), 34.

the hope of heaven was the force that carried these people through excruciating labor and atrocious oppression. Heaven consumed the whole of their personhood in a manner that drove and sustained their courageous lives. We are hoping for God to perform similar transformation in our lives to that of these faithful believers.

The more we live with our heads on a heavenly swivel, thinking about the endpoint, calling to mind heaven and the second coming of Christ, the more heavenward our lives will move. The more heavenward we become, the more eternity will naturally drive our actions and comfort our hearts.

Top-Down and Bottom-Up Heavenwardness

The hope of our heavenly sanctification is that as we love Jesus more and more, our hearts and minds will increasingly turn to heaven. Jesus is the center of our heavenly home. Therefore, an interrelatedness exists between growing in Christ and increasing in heavenwardness. To love Jesus is to long to feel closer to him. To love Jesus is to long to see him. Since heaven involves optimal intimacy with Christ and the full vision of Christ, the natural momentum of the maturing believer moves toward eternity. To this end, Puritan theologian Jeremiah Burroughs wrote:

> I remember it was written of Queen Mary, that she said if they ripped her open they would find tea in her heart. And so it may be said of saints whose conversation is in heaven, who walk with God and live here lives of heaven upon earth, if they were ripped open, you would find heaven in their hearts.[2]

2 Jeremiah Burroughs, *Two Treatises of Mr. Jeremiah Burroughs* (Ligonier, PA: Soli Deo Gloria, 1991), 98.

Imagine having this heavenly consumption of which Burroughs speaks! Imagine eternity permeating your whole being. Imagine the perspective, the patience, and the clarity you would have. Burroughs could simultaneously say that these saints' hearts were filled with Jesus, since Christ is the center of heaven. For the Christian, being consumed with heaven necessarily means being consumed with Jesus. To long to be in heaven is to long to be with Christ.

With Paul, his heavenwardness operated in both a bottom-up and a top-down posture. When Paul wrote about a matter in life and then instinctively related it to heaven, this exhibited his bottom-up posture. He would begin with a specific matter and then relate it to the general principles of eternity. For example, in 1 Corinthians Paul rebuked the church for an incident of gross sexual immorality (1 Cor. 5:1–5). After reprimanding them, he exhorted the church to restore this particular member to godliness so "that his spirit may be saved in the day of the Lord" (5:5). He connected his admonitions of repentance and moral purity to the condition of the sinner at the day of Christ. It's not simply a "be good now" mentality; he had eternity in mind. The specific matter of sexual immorality was related to the general principles of eternity, namely, the final judgment.

Paul also thought in a top-down manner, when he ruminated on heaven, and that meditation then translated into practical insights related to life. In this way he started with the general principles of eternity and then moved down to the consideration of specific matters.

In 2 Timothy, Paul started by charging Timothy "in the presence of God and of Christ Jesus, who is to judge the living and the dead, and by his appearing and his kingdom: preach the word; be ready in season and out of season; reprove, rebuke, and exhort, with complete patience and teaching" (2 Tim. 4:1–2). His conception of seeing Christ at his final appearing informed the way the pastor should think about preaching. This perspective, in effect, led him to communicate to Timothy, "Ministry and preaching are weighty business. Take it seriously." The awareness of seeing God in his holiness at his appearing (the general principle of eternity) quickened the focus and gravity with which he considered preaching (the specific matter).

Church father Gregory of Nyssa exhibited this top-down heavenward posture in relation to worship and prayer. Gregory pondered heavenly beings constantly praising the Lord above in his glory:

> When I hear of the altar of offering and the altar of incense, I understand the adoration of the heavenly beings which is perpetually offered in this tabernacle, for he says that not only the tongues of those on earth and in the underworld but also of those in the heavens render praise to the beginnings of all things. This is the sacrifice pleasing to God, a verbal sacrifice, as the Apostle says, the fragrance of prayer.[3]

Gregory's consideration of the worship of God in heaven (general principle of eternity) shaped the way he thought about praying to and praising the Lord (specific matter). It moved him to want to offer his life as a living sacrifice.

Whether it took on a bottom-up or top-down nature, heaven is above, below, and within the way Paul viewed the world. It saturated his perspective to the point that when asking the Philippians to help Clement and his other ministry partners, he referred to

---

3 Gregory of Nyssa, *The Life of Moses* (New York: Paulist Press, 1978), 101.

them as those "whose names are in the book of life" (Phil. 4:3). With all deference to the apostle Paul, this is a somewhat bizarre way to identify people. Nevertheless, this reference shows just how much heaven dominated Paul's consciousness. The apostle certainly felt bound together with these (geographically) far-away friends through the knowledge of their mutual citizenship in heaven. In both the top-down and botton-up examples, the common thread is a heart and mind anchored in glory such that the moment of the believer's life is always moving heavenward.

If you're a single person earnestly desiring a spouse, wondering when God will give you this gift can understandably cause pain. And in the midst of that longing and lament, how much does a heavenly consumption and your eternal marriage to Christ in heaven grant you patience?

When you lose perspective about worldly matters such as possessions and achievements, how does a persistent awareness that you will inherit the earth with Christ enable you to let go of these materialistic fixations and repent from that idolatry? When you think about the trillions of years we have in the new heavens and new earth, does it slow you down a step or two? When you envision Christ on his heavenly throne when tempted to enter defensively into a trivial argument, how much does it relax you and enable you to refrain from a potentially damaging debate?

A heavenward soul frees you. It settles you down. It grants you patience and comfort. It transforms you.

Heavenward Passivity

So far I have characterized the heavenward life in active terms with a forward momentum. However, there's a third posture of the heavenward life revealed in this one emblematic word: *waiting*. In Titus, Paul taught how the grace of God had come to save us and teach us to live "godly lives in the present age, *waiting* for our blessed hope, the appearing of the glory of our great God and Savior Jesus Christ" (Titus 2:12–13). A concurrence exists in this verse and in the Christian life. We strive to honor and glorify God through godly, loving lives by his grace. Simultaneously, we actively wait for Christ's return.

Paul referred to the Christian life in a similar manner in 1 Corinthians. He expressed gratitude for the grace God gave these believers to sustain them so that they were not lacking in any gift, as they waited for the revealing of the Lord Jesus Christ (1 Cor. 1:7). We live our lives. We depend on grace. All the while, though, we actively wait for heaven.

We are enjoying life, we are working, we are serving, we are struggling, and all the while we are waiting to get home.

Waiting carries unpleasant connotations for most of us. We hate waiting in lines or in traffic. Waiting for a delayed flight frustrates us, while waiting for a license renewal at the DMV drives us insane! At a much more serious level, waiting for God to bless us with a spouse or a baby can be painful.

But there are kinds of waiting that bring us joy. An engaged bride and groom feel so much excitement and happiness as they count down the days until their wedding. Sports fans read blogs, listen to podcasts, and talk about their favorite team as they wait for kickoff or opening day of their favorite sport. These types of waiting are still tough because they involve unsatisfied longing for a period of time, but the waiting also brings us joyful anticipation.

Waiting for heaven and for the second coming of Christ is this joyful type of waiting. Won't it be glorious to be with him? Won't it be wonderful to be healed of our wounds and our sorrows? Won't it be amazing never to worry or fear again? Won't it be incredible to see the glorious majesty of Jesus, the source of all beauty? I can hardly stand it!

The heavenward life on offer to us through the Spirit involves the concurrence of a faithful struggle to persevere in godly, loving lives while simultaneously waiting expectantly to be with our King. This glorious waiting provides a buoyancy and positivity that only support our desire and ability to glorify God in our lives and to persevere in hard times. Heavenward waiting stabilizes us in a way that grants comfort and hope.

Your Heavenward Journey

With heavenly mindedness we make an intentional effort to set our mind "on things above." In the heavenward life, though, heaven becomes an organic part of our hearts, minds, and actions.

Heaven became the air that Paul breathed. We all can long for such a heavenward posture in our lives. Patience, comfort, and hope arise when we consider heaven as the horizon of our mindset and eternity as the basis of our sense of time.

Growing heavenward begins with increasing in your knowledge of heaven. Reading books about heaven, studying the book of Revelation, and paying attention to heavenly references in Scripture are good practical steps. We can play our part in this manner.

Ultimately, though, the Lord has to transform us to integrate heaven into our hearts and minds such that eternity seeps into our whole personhood. Puritan theologian John Owen wrote:

By [hope] we are purified, sanctified, saved. And to sum up the whole of its excellency and efficacy, it is a principal way of the working of Christ as inhabiting in us: Colossians 1:27: "Christ in you, the hope of glory." Where Christ evidences his presence with us, he give us an infallible hope of glory; he gives us an assured pledge of it, and worketh our souls unto an expectation of it.[4]

Owen discusses how Christ (specifically Christ in our hearts) works to cultivate a heavenly longing in our souls and an eternal mindset. We can grow in the heavenward life through diligence in scriptural study, but we ultimately pray to the Holy Spirit to turn our minds and affections above. We trust him to make eternity seep into hearts and minds.

When the Spirit does this work, heaven permeates our whole being in such a way that eternity almost subliminally and instinctively drives and shapes our lives. Through the Spirit, heaven becomes such a central and natural aspect of our perspective that we don't even deliberately think about it: heaven is simply the air that *we* breath. It's always top of mind and heart. For example, when you are sitting on a plane and the conversation with a nonbeliever turns to spiritual matters, the realities of heaven move you to share the gospel. You instinctively recognize the eternal stakes of this person's life. The weight of eternity enables you to overcome the fears of rejection and the discomfort of awkwardness and to offer the good news.

If you are a workaholic parent who constantly lives with the notion that you will start prioritizing your marriage and kids once

4   John Owen, *Sin and Grace*, vol. 7, *The Works of John Owen* (London: Banner of Truth, 1965), 321–22.

you get over the next horizon, heaven persistently reminds you of the shortness of earthly life. The consistent awareness of just how long eternity is awakens you to just how short the years are that your children live in your home. Eighteen years compared to the daily backdrop of eternity wakes you up from the delusion that your window of influence on your kids is never-ending. Eternal time spurs earthly urgency. It compels you to repent from the idol of work, to create some boundaries, and to put time with your family first.

If you are a person who gets tied in knots over trivial things, eternity can enable you to chill out. With heaven as the backdrop, you can gain perspective and turn down the temperature by asking the question, "Will this really matter in eternity?"

Although it is extremely painful, my son's presence in heaven naturally supports this transformation. As I miss him and yearn to be with him, my heart and mind naturally turn upward. My son's life in glory put my heart and mind on the heavenly swivel. My longing for the person made me long for the place as well.

For any believer, our longing for Christ inherently turns our soul heavenward. We desire to see him and to be with him. We yearn for our soul to be fully satisfied by perfect, heavenly communion with him. Our whole self lives on a swivel, constantly turning to Jesus and his heavenly glory.

As our hearts and minds move in this direction, and as we pray for the Lord to grant us an eternal mindset, Christ can do a work to our hearts and from within our hearts to give us a heavenward perspective that truly transforms our lives.

WHY PAUL WAS SO HEAVENWARD (AND YOU CAN BE TOO!)

3

The Arrival of Heaven

The Christ Event

YOU CANNOT UNDERSTAND why Paul was so heavenward unless you first understand what the Christ Event represented to the apostle. When you realize the massive heavenly implications of the coming of Christ, your life will move in a heavenward direction. Understanding these implications requires comprehending the significance of the season in which you live.

When putting on a play, there are phases leading up to opening night. The first phase involves practice. The actors receive their lines, read them, and begin to memorize them. They have rehearsals where they practice lines and movements and songs until they get every detail right. The dress rehearsal is the next step. The stakes rise from practice. A small audience may watch. Some room exists for mistakes, but the dress rehearsal entails greater intensity than practice. Finally comes opening night and the live performance phase. Every actress and actor is completely focused. If someone has an illness, he powers through in order to participate in what he's invested so much in. The acting company may perform multiple times in this phase. In each performance, all players give maximal effort and attention because they know the significance of this phase.

The phase of the process impacts everything. It makes all the difference.

For Paul, the coming of Jesus marked the dawn of a new phase of redemptive history. As the end of the dress rehearsal marks the segue to the live performance phase, the first coming of Christ marked the beginning of the second to last chapter in redemptive history, the season of heaven on earth.

In this chapter, you will see the four critical signs, associated with the coming of Christ, which alerted Paul that this new glorious season had arrived for all of us.

Paul and Old Testament Expectations

In grammar we have punctuation marks to signify the end of a sentence. Whether it's a period, a question mark, or an exclamation point, that mark communicates that one thought has ended and a new thought will begin.

In Christianity, the punctuation mark to which we look is the second coming of Christ. This moment will mark the end of the present evil age and the beginning of the long-expected period, the new heaven and the new earth (another way of saying "heaven on earth.") In the Old Testament, the Jews looked to and called the punctuation mark "the day of the Lord." They referred to the period after the day of the Lord as "the age to come," which is essentially the same thing as the new heaven and new earth.

George Ladd defined the day of the Lord as "a day of divine visitation when God will come in judgment and salvation to establish his Kingdom."[1] The Old Testament's depictions of this day paint a terrifying picture of judgment. The prophet Zephaniah refers to it as "a day of wrath . . . of distress and anguish . . . of ruin and devastation . . . of darkness and gloom . . . of clouds and thick darkness . . . of trumpet blast and battle cry" (Zeph. 1:15–16). This description does not portray the day of the Lord as some positive, hopeful moment to anticipate. However, on this day, God will come to earth, rid the world of evil, and purify the earth in such a manner that the age to come, heaven on earth, is ushered in. Thus, the day of the Lord bisects the two eras in the Jewish conception of redemptive history: the present evil age and the age to come.

Much content related to the day of the Lord runs throughout the major and minor prophets of the Old Testament. Through this content, Jews developed certain expectations of the day. They looked for certain signs that would signal its arrival. In the same way that Americans look for temperatures to drop and the leaves to turn golden and orange to signal the dawn of autumn, *Jews were looking for four particular supernatural signs to occur to demonstrate the arrival of the Lord God on earth*. These four signs are critical to understanding why Paul asserts that the age to come has arrived through Christ.

The first sign involved a *divine visitation*. Malachi asked, "Who can endure the day of his coming, and who can stand when he appears? For he is like a refiner's fire and like fullers' soap" (Mal. 3:2).

---

1   George Ladd, *Theology of the New Testament* (Grand Rapids, MI: Eerdmans, 1993), 602.

In that same passage God declares, "Then I will draw near to you for judgment" (3:5). At the core, Jews expected God himself to come to earth in his full glory on that day.

A second sign was the *resurrection of the dead.* Jews anticipated that all people—the faithful and unfaithful alike—would rise from the grave in a bodily form at the day of the Lord. Daniel prophesied that during the last days, "Many of those who sleep in the dust of the earth shall awake, some to everlasting life, and some to shame and everlasting contempt" (Dan. 12:2). A significant part of the Jewish eschatological consciousness involved the expectation of a universal resurrection of the body at the end.

A third sign, closely related to divine visitation, was *divine judgment.* Admonitions of judgment and retribution comprise the most prominent aspect of the day of the Lord. Jeremiah referred to it as a "day of vengeance" (Jer. 46:10), and Isaiah called it a day of "wrath and fierce anger" (Isa. 13:9). The prophetic literature of the Old Testament depicted it as a day when God would strike down his enemies and judge all sin.

The fourth and final sign of the day of the Lord entailed an *outpouring of the Holy Spirit.* The prophet Joel predicted:

> And it shall come to pass afterward,
>   that I will pour out my Spirit on all flesh;
> your sons and your daughters shall prophesy,
>   your old men shall dream dreams,
>   and your young men shall see visions.
> Even on the male and female servants
>   in those days I will pour out my Spirit.

And I will show wonders in the heavens and on the earth, blood and fire and columns of smoke. The sun shall be turned to darkness, and the moon to blood, *before the great and awesome day of the LORD comes.* (Joel 2:28–31)

Geerhardus Vos wrote that this pouring out of the Spirit and other supernatural signs "heralds the fast approach of the future world."[2]

These four signs created a checklist of sorts to which a faithful Jew would look in anticipation of the day of the Lord. With this checklist of indicators marking the arrival of the day of the Lord, we now can better understand Paul's shocking conversion and radical declaration that the day had arrived, that the age to come is now, and that heaven, indeed, is a place on earth.

The Checking of the Boxes of Paul's Conversion

Many people have had a single moment, a supernatural occasion, when their life turned on a dime. For you, a tragedy, a birth, a diagnosis, an opportunity, an accident, or a current event may have radically shifted the course of your life. For Paul, this "turn on a dime" moment happened on the road to Damascus. At that time, he was known as the devout Jew, Saul, who passionately opposed Christianity and actively persecuted believers. However, on the road to Damascus, Paul's life, name, and view of reality radically shifted.

On this road, "a light from heaven shone around him" and a voiced called out to Saul, asking, "Saul, Saul, why are you persecuting me?" Saul's response demonstrates that this was no

2   Geerhardus Vos, *The Pauline Eschatology* (Grand Rapids, MI: Eerdmans, 1953), 160.

ordinary light. He fell to the ground and questioned, "Who are you, Lord?" (Acts 9:3–4). Based on his prostrate response and the one whom he addresses, it's clear that Saul knew he had encountered God himself.

In response to Saul's question, Jesus identified himself as the voice. From here, the boxes of the redemptive historic checklist began to be checked. The light came on. The scales fell off his blinded eyes. Everything changed.

The first change was his name: Saul became Paul. Then Paul was immediately baptized. He went directly to the synagogue and declared, "[Jesus] is the Son of God" (Acts 9:20). The persecutor of Christians inexplicably and instantly became the proclaimer of Christ.

What happened? Did Jesus deliver a doctrinal lecture or lesson to Saul? Did he hand him a book? No. Two pivotal things occurred.

First, Paul grasped that Jesus Christ was, in fact, God Almighty. This realization meant that the Lord God had come to earth in the incarnation of Jesus. Box 1 of the day of the Lord checklist, *a divine visitation*, had been checked.

Second, Jesus appeared to Paul in his resurrected body. Paul had an opportunity to witness the risen Christ with his own two eyes. Regarding this, Richard Gaffin wrote, "[Jesus's] resurrection is the representative beginning of the resurrection of believers."[3] In other words, in a partial sense, the anticipated resurrection of the dead has occurred in the resurrection of Jesus. The rest of the resurrection harvest will occur at the second coming of Christ,

---

3   Richard B. Gaffin Jr., *Resurrection and Redemption: A Study in Paul's Soteriology* (Phillipsburg, NJ: P&R, 1987), 34.

but Paul had witnessed the "firstfruits" of that harvest on the road to Damascus. Box 2 in the day of the Lord checklist had been marked.

As stated earlier, a central expectation associated with the day of the Lord involved a final, divine judgment, which represents box 3. The apostle viewed the death of Jesus on the cross as the first installment of the final judgment of God. In Romans 3:25, he refers to the death of Christ as a "propitiation," meaning a sacrifice that receives the wrath of God for the atonement of believers. Herman Ridderbos says that in the same way that Christ's resurrection was a foretaste of the future resurrection of the dead, the cross was a foretaste of the final judgment, which also will occur at the second coming of Christ: "Just as Christ's resurrection is the breaking through of the new creation, so the final judgment of God has become manifest in his death."[4]

In plain language, Ridderbos says that the cross of Jesus has big-picture importance as well; it checks box 3. God's final judgment has been executed in the past. However, his Son Jesus absorbed this divine judgment for God's people. This does not just carry historic significance for our intellectual delight. This means that if you are a believer in Christ, your final judgment has already occurred; it is in the rearview mirror of your life.

In Galatians 3:14 Paul referred to the "promised Spirit." The promise to which he refers is that of the outpouring of the Holy Spirit, as predicted in Old Testament prophets. The Pentecost of Acts 2 marks in history the coming down of the Spirit, the initial installment of this "day of the Lord" promise.

4   Herman Ridderbos, *Paul: An Outline of His Theology* (Grand Rapids, MI: Eerdmans, 1998), 167.

To Paul the outpouring of the Holy Spirit has even greater implications than simply checking box 4. The manifestation and reality of the complete rule and full presence of God follows the day of the Lord. God's presence and rule on earth constitute a core benefit and characteristic of the new heavens and new earth. The outpouring of the Holy Spirit means the beginning of this expected manifestation of the rule and presence of God on earth. It will culminate fully at the second coming of Christ, but this partial manifestation of his rule has come via the arrival of the Spirit.

For Paul and for us, all of the "day of the Lord" boxes were checked, which means something extraordinarily significant.

Heaven Is, in Fact, a Place on Earth

With all four boxes checked, Paul makes a radical declaration throughout his letters: the day of the Lord has occurred! The age to come is upon us. Heaven has come to earth.

Paul cites the prophetic promise of Isaiah 49:8 in 2 Corinthians 6:2: "In a favorable time I listened to you, and in a day of salvation I have helped you." He then connects this verse to the present age into which Christ has come: "Behold, now is the favorable time; behold, now is the day of salvation." The future age to come is now.

He makes this remark in a different manner in Galatians, when he writes, "When the *fullness of time* had come, God sent forth his Son, born of woman, born under the law, to redeem those who were under the law, so that we might receive adoption as sons" (Gal. 4:4–5). At just the right time, according to God's plans and purposes, Christ came, bringing the future heavenly age into the present. This means that heavenly realities no longer exist exclusively in the future; they exist in our lives. George Ladd sums it up by saying:

> [The realities of heaven] are not merely detached events lying in the future about which Paul speculates. They are rather preemptive events that have already begun to unfold within history. The blessings of the Age to Come no longer lie exclusively in the future; they have become objects of present experience.[5]

As we've noted, in the first century, people most frequently referred to the future heavenly era as "the age to come." In this book I sometimes refer to it as "the new heavenly age" as a way to emphasize the heavenly aspect of the time in which we live. In his letters, Paul talks about the presence of the age to come with three primary realities. (Each of these paradigms has different characteristics, but they all communicate the same thing: heaven has come to earth.)

When we know these heavenly realities, we can see just how much heaven pervades Paul's everyday perspective and just how gloriously heaven can integrate into our lives.

Paradigm 1: New Creation

People often use the term *born-again Christian* to refer to converted believers. Being "born again" fits well with Paul's paradigm of the new creation.

Paul famously wrote in 2 Corinthians 5:17, "If anyone is in Christ, he is a new creation." Paul views the resurrection of Christ as the inception of the new creation. As Jesus rises from the dead in

---

5 Ladd, *Theology of the New Testament*, 596.

a new, glorified body, he represents the firstfruits and first evidence of the future fulfillment of the new heaven and new earth. In the spiritual sense, the new creation has sprung forth and exists. It only awaits its physical consummation, as evidenced in creation's longing and groaning (Rom. 8; 2 Cor. 5).

Only twice does Paul explicitly use the term *new creation* (2 Cor. 5:17; Gal. 6:15). However, Paul uses different terms within this category. In Romans 5 and 1 Corinthians 15, Paul refers to Jesus as the new Adam. In this way, Jesus is the first person to live in the new creation. The old, fallen Adam served as the head of the original creation; Jesus, the second Adam, is the head of the new creation. In Colossians 1 Paul's references to Christ as the "firstborn from the dead" and "firstborn of all creation" speaks to his primacy in the new creation (Col. 1:18, 15).

The verbs Paul uses related to creating often signal that he is speaking of heavenly realities related to the new creation. In Ephesians 2:10 Paul writes that believers were "created in Christ Jesus for good works." Christians are born anew into the new creation where they live to do good works through the power of the Holy Spirit.

Finally, when Paul uses the adjective "new" in 2 Corinthians 5:17, this can signify that he is talking about realities of the new creation. For example, in Colossians 3:9–10 he reminds believers that they have "put off the old self with its practices and have put on the new self, which is being renewed in knowledge after the image of its creator." Believers have been transferred to the new creation and should live according to the new self in that place. The Creator, in whose image they are being renewed, is Christ, the new Adam of the new creation.

The new creation emphasizes the newness of the new heavenly age and the break from the old to the new. There's an encouragement for us in realizing that through faith we no longer live under Adam as our fallen head but under Christ, the risen Lord, who renews all things.

Paradigm 2: The Age of the Spirit

Most often when people see the word *Spirit* in Paul's writing, they believe that he is exclusively referring to the work of the Holy Spirit in the lives of individuals. At times, Paul means something similar but different. Paul will use the term *Spirit* in heavenly terms, representing the new heavenly age. This usage is particularly obvious when Paul talks about the Spirit in opposition to the flesh. In these circumstances, these two words represent two different and contrary eschatological ages.

Ridderbos asserts that the Spirit and the flesh are the "two dominating principles of the two aeons marked off by the appearance of Christ."[6] In Romans, Paul speaks in these terms often. In Romans 7:6 Paul writes, "But now we are released from the law, having died to that which held us captive, so that we serve in the new way of the Spirit and not in the old way of the written code." Then in Romans 8:5 he says, "For those who live according to the flesh set their minds on the things of the flesh, but those who live according to the Spirit set their minds on the things of the Spirit." In these texts, the Spirit represents the new way of living in this heavenly age. One walks by faith out of the power of the indwelling Holy Spirit and no longer by the power of human effort.

6   Ridderbos, *Paul*, 215.

This paradigm dedicates particular attention to the activity of the Holy Spirit in the new heavenly age. The Spirit empowers the redemptive activity of God through the lives of believers in the new heavenly age, bringing about new life and new fruit.

Paradigm 3: The Kingdom

A third major category that Paul uses to depict the new heavenly age is that of the kingdom of God. The kingdom of God constitutes the primary paradigm used in the Synoptic Gospels to announce the inception of the age to come through Christ's life, death, and resurrection.[7] Paul uses it less frequently than the Gospel writers, but George Ladd writes that "[Paul] does frequently speak of the eschatological Kingdom of God."[8]

Paul refers to Jesus as "Lord" ninety times. When Paul alludes to Jesus in this manner, it reflects his acknowledgment of Jesus as the King of the kingdom of God. Paul writes in 2 Corinthians 3:17, "Now the Lord is the Spirit, and where the Spirit of the Lord is, there is freedom." He conceives of Jesus as the reigning King of the new heavenly age, who carries out his rule through the activity of the Spirit.

In Colossians 1:13 Paul describes conversion as being "delivered . . . from the domain of darkness and transferred . . . to the kingdom of his beloved Son." Here "kingdom" represents being transferred to a new realm, the heavenly age to come. In three different circumstances

---

7   The kingdom of God has both present and future connotations. In one sense, "the kingdom" refers to the presence of God's visible rule, as heaven has partially come to earth. In another sense, it has future connotations as the future reality of the consummation of God's redemptive work at the second coming, when God's kingdom fully comes to earth.

8   Ladd, *Theology of the New Testament*, 403.

Paul discusses someone not "inheriting the kingdom of God" because of sinful living. Paul, of course, does not suggest that salvation comes by works, since faith is the means by which a person enters the age to come. Since we have sinful flesh, of course we will continue to sin. However, Paul does say that a person who truly dwells in the kingdom of God will demonstrate the ethical fruit of a believer.

This paradigm gives us direction in how we live as residents of the new heavenly age. We live ethical lives that reflect the lifestyle of those in glory.

Heaven Has Come but Let's Not Go Too Far: Already and Not Yet

Danger can arise when we mention the entrance of heaven into this earth. We can forget that the present evil age has not concluded. We can presume that the present benefits and joys of the new heavenly age mean perpetual happiness now and the absence of difficulty. Sin, death, and the devil still afflict us. Pain, suffering, and injustice still cause pain.

We presently live in a unique time known as "the already and the not yet," which involves the overlapping of two ages. Christ has already defeated sin, death, and the devil. The kingdom of heaven has *already* come to earth. However, God has *not yet* eradicated the world from the pains of the fall, the presence of wickedness, or the brokenness of sin. The Lord will eliminate those things at the second coming of Christ, when the present evil age will conclude. Until then, the darkness of the present evil age intermingles with the joys of heaven on earth.

What does this mean for us? This means that we should pursue the joys of the current heavenly realities all around us while maintaining reasonable expectations for life on this earth. We will continue to sin, get hurt, and witness evil. However, we have the hope and comfort that these pains are temporary, as we drink in, sip by sip, the eternal pleasures of our salvation.

Your Heavenward Journey

When my son passed away, the deepest part of my sorrow involved the separation I experienced. I wanted so deeply to feel connected to him. And yet he was in heaven, and I am stuck here on earth. Heaven can feel so far away and distant when we call it to mind. We think of Christ on his throne in the heavenly realms. This sense of distance makes that sorrow of separation hurt that much more. I experienced comfort knowing that my son, Cam, sat at the feet of Christ and saw him face-to-face, but still, I wanted to be with him, and he felt so far away.

The core fundamental of heaven on earth gave me immense comfort in this grief. Paul writes in 2 Corinthians 5:17, "If anyone is in Christ, he is a new creation." The term "in Christ" signifies union with Christ, that Christ dwells in our hearts as we dwell in his. We are one with Christ. The center of heaven on earth is union with Christ. To be in the new creation is to be in union with Christ. To be in heaven above with God is to be in union with Christ as well. The tie that binds me to my son and my son to me is Christ and our mutual union with him.

I have often thought that Cam and I are both simultaneously hugging the same massive oak tree. He stands on one side and I the other. The girth of the tree is so immense that we cannot see each other. Nevertheless, we grip that oak tree with the same joy, affection, and pleasure.

In reality, the oak tree is Jesus. The Jesus in my soul is the same Jesus in Cam's soul. He dwells in the heart of Christ as I dwell in the heart of Christ. We are simultaneously embracing the same Jesus, who binds us together.

I've said that what makes heaven *heaven* is being with Jesus. This remains consistent with heaven on earth. Jesus's presence in your heart constitutes the core blessing of heaven on earth.

As we grieve, nothing will make us feel more connected with our loved ones above than feeling connected to Jesus. When we cling to Christ, we are hugging the same oak tree that our loved ones in heaven embrace above.

As you pursue heavenly mindedness, understand that delighting in your union with Christ and cultivating intimacy with him are the primary ways you taste pleasures of heaven here and now.

4

The Entrance to Heaven

Conversion

LOCATION SHAPES US. The place in which we dwell influences our speech, customs, preferences, and worldview.

I have lived in the heart of the American South—Birmingham, Alabama—for all but four of my forty-two years. As a result, I say things like "Y'all," "Yes, ma'am," and "No, sir." I stand when a person comes to the table at a restaurant. I follow college football instead of the NFL, and I think barbecue means pork, not brisket—and definitely not burgers.

When I moved to Wake Forest University in North Carolina for college, though, some things about me changed. My professors were not all that keen on my calling them sir and ma'am. Some women took offense to my standing when they came to the table at a restaurant, viewing it as demeaning or chauvinistic. I gained a heightened interest in ACC basketball and NASCAR for the first time. Vinegar-based barbecue pork became my favorite version. My location and its culture shaped me in particular ways. A transfer from Alabama to Wake Forest resulted in some personal transformations.

Not only does location shape the way we live; it also affects our mood. Certain places bring us happiness. I feel alive when I sip coffee on a breezy spring or fall day on the brick sidewalk outside of Continental Bakery. I have this divine sense of serenity when I sit among the canopy of trees on the elevated back porch of my family's North Carolina mountain house. I feel electricity when I emerge from the tunnel and see one hundred thousand people in an SEC football stadium. The second I arrive in these places, my heart elevates. The place shapes the mood.

For the apostle Paul, the partial coming of the day of the Lord and the age to come (discussed in the previous chapter) not only constituted a new era but also the establishment of a new spiritual place. In a similar light salvation for Paul did not simply involve forgiveness of sins and receiving the righteousness of God through faith. Certainly these two blessings serve as the core of conversion, but for Paul salvation also involved a massive, cosmic transfer from one place to another. The fact of a believer's transfer from an old location to a new one completely transformed the way he viewed the world.

For Paul, prior to conversion we dwelled in the "domain of darkness" (Col. 1:13), where we were spiritually dead, following the prince of the air, and living as children of wrath (Eph. 2:1–3). However, through the work of Christ we have radically changed locations. Paul writes to the Colossians, "[God] has delivered us from the domain of darkness and transferred us to the kingdom of his beloved Son, in whom we have redemption, the forgiveness of sins" (Col. 1:13). Not only does Christ save us from our sins, but also he saves us from a location of darkness and transfers us into a new place: the realm of heaven.

Paul's reference to the "kingdom of his beloved Son" takes on heavenly implications. As we mentioned in chapter 3, Paul uses several paradigms to describe the reality of heaven having come to earth. Here in Colossians 1 Paul alludes to the kingdom of heaven as a place of current residence for the believer *in this life*, not just upon death.

This transfer of spiritual location, from the domain of darkness to the heavenly kingdom of God's Son, may constitute the single biggest factor in Paul's heavenward transformation.

You may have lived for many years as a believer and been totally unaware of this transfer! Before I began my journey with Paul after my son's death, I did not realize this seismic aspect of my salvation. Awakening to this spiritual reality had a life-changing impact on my life moving heavenward, and I think it will in yours too as you see the impact that naturally occurs when we realize our transfer to a new location, the kingdom of heaven.

Citizens of Heaven

Philippians may be Paul's most heaven-saturated letter, with over a dozen references to glory. Most likely, Paul was in a heavenly state of mind when he sat down to write this letter due to the possibility of imminent death.

The theological anchor of this deeply eschatological book comes in Philippians 3:20–21, where Paul declares, "Our citizenship is in heaven, and from it we await a Savior, the Lord Jesus Christ, who will transform our lowly body to be like his glorious body, by the power that enables him even to subject all things to himself."

The term *citizenship* carried weighty connotations in the Roman world, and particularly in Philippi. The Philippians prided themselves on being a Roman colony. The Greek term for *citizenship* often connoted a person living abroad from their native land and was even used to refer to an exile. While the Philippians may have dwelled hundreds of miles away from the Roman epicenter, they still believed that they had a home in Rome. They physically dwelled, worked, and carried on their lives in Philippi, but in their hearts Rome was, in some sense, home base.

Paul exhibited this mentality in the book of Acts. After he was arrested in Jerusalem, the government wanted to try him there. However, Paul protested, asserting that he was a Roman citizen, and exercised his right to "appeal to Caesar" (Acts 25:11–12). Therefore, he had a right to a trial in Rome. Paul never owned a residence in Rome, but he possessed the rights and benefits of a Roman citizen. Consequently, Festus, the Roman governor of Judea, sent Paul to Rome to stand trial.

Along these same lines Paul told the Philippians that their true citizenship was in heaven. He did not refer to their heavenly citizenship as a future reality but as a present one. Heaven *is* your current spiritual home. When he talked about waiting for Christ to return, he said, "From it we await a Savior, the Lord Jesus Christ." The "it" refers to heaven. Think about this: Paul says "from heaven" we wait for our Savior to come to us on earth to "transform our lowly [bodies]." (This is pretty confusing, right?)

While heaven constitutes our spiritual home, our bodies still bond us to the fallen world. In a sense, through the first coming of Christ and through our conversion, we have the initial blessing of heavenly citizenship. This initial blessing only fuels our hunger and longing for the consummation of the heavenly life, which occurs when we meet Jesus face-to-face, either in heaven or at the second coming of Christ. We eagerly wait for that day.

The Philippians lived physically on earth, but their true dwelling was heaven. With this metaphor of heavenly citizenship Paul reinforced this top-down orientation for believers. In other words, Paul wanted Christians to consider heaven their true dwelling place and view their lives on earth from that up-above perspective. Paul's assertion of heavenly citizenship obviously extends beyond the Philippians to all believers. Paul is making a declaration about your *current* (yes, right now!*)* and true home: heaven.

The apostle's exhortation, however, went beyond just a location and resultant mindset. The concept of citizenship fell within the larger Greco-Roman category of the *polis*, or city. The concept of citizenship was more than just a national or cultural identification. Citizens of a nation were expected to carry and further the customs of the motherland to the place they inhabited.[1] Gordon Fee described this expectation in this manner: "Just as Philippi was a colony of Rome, whose citizens thereby exemplified the life of Rome in the province of Macedonia, so the citizens of the 'Heavenly Commonwealth' were to function as a colony of heaven in that outpost of Rome."[2]

Because of this present dwelling in heaven, Paul encouraged believers not just to think with a heavenly mindset but also to carry the values, beliefs, and customs of heaven into the world.

---

1 Gerhard Kittel, Gerhard Friedrich, and Geoffrey William Bromiley, *Theological Dictionary of the New Testament* (Grand Rapids, MI: Eerdmans, 1985), s.v. "citizenship."

2 Cited in Stephen J. Nichols, *Heaven On Earth: Capturing Jonathan Edwards's Vision of Living in Between* (Wheaton, IL: Crossway, 2006), 47.

The new heavenly place should naturally result in a heavenward life. Therefore, the place should shape the person, and then the person should shape the place.

One figure who embodied the heavenly centered mentality was pastor and theologian Jonathan Edwards. Edwards was one of the most significant figures in the history of American Christianity. He was a prolific writer and influential leader who endured much trial and suffering in his life. Heaven comprised one of the major themes in his writing and preaching. Author Stephen Nichols described Edwards as one "consumed by heaven." He says that Edwards's "vision of the church consisted of a redeemed community living in this life according to the principles and dictates of the life to come."[3]

Both Edwards and Paul envisioned themselves as truly dwelling in heaven and then translated their lives on earth through this lens. They maintained a top-down mentality. Paul's exhortations for Christians to live with a heavenly mindset flow out of this perspective.

As you internalize your heavenly citizenship, there is the hope and possibility that you can live with this same type of top-down view of the world. You can see yourself as a citizen of glory carrying out the customs, beliefs, and practices of heaven on earth.

The Before and After of the New Heavenly Place

As I referenced earlier, one could observe differences in me during my four years at Wake Forest. A "before and after" difference occurred as a result of place. Throughout his letters, we can observe

---

3 Nichols, *Heaven on Earth*, 24.

similar "before and after" realities of life in a person's salvation. In 2 Corinthians 5:16–18 Paul wrote:

> From now on, therefore, we regard no one according to the flesh. Even though we once regarded Christ according to the flesh, we regard him thus no longer. Therefore, if anyone is in Christ, he is a new creation. The old has passed away; behold, the new has come. All this is from God, who through Christ reconciled us to himself and gave us the ministry of reconciliation.

Paul's reference to the flesh has eschatological connotations. Those in "the flesh" are the people residing in the kingdom of darkness. He no longer regards people from a viewpoint of the old age or the old place; he now sees the world through the lens of the new creation, the realm of heaven. If any person is in union with Christ, then he now dwells in the new creation, the new heavenly place. Is he, at the individual level, a new creation? Yes, indeed. But this individual transformation follows the spiritual transfer from the old age to the new creation, the kingdom of heaven.

Paul finishes this thought, in 2 Corinthians 5:18, by addressing how God reconciled sinners to Jesus. We were far away from Christ, living in the domain of darkness, but now God has brought us into Christ. Where does Christ dwell? Well, everywhere, but specifically in heaven at the right hand of the Father. Where have we been brought? Into Christ. The point to glean from this challenging truth is that Christ is the center of our new heavenly place. We dwell in the new location through our union with Christ and in his heart.

As a result of this new orientation, Paul states that God has given us the "ministry of reconciliation" (5:18). Having been brought into the new creation by reconciliation, Christ compels us to share the gospel with others so that they may dwell in the new place too. This reality creates a new mindset for evangelism. You can now think, "I live here in a new heavenly place under the rule of Christ. Let me invite others to join me in this place by telling them about reconciliation with God through Christ."

In 2 Corinthians 5, Paul demonstrates two changes that the new location, the new creation, initiates. First, the way we view the world changes. We no longer think in earthly terms but instead in heavenly terms. Furthermore, understanding how the Father brought us into the new creation through the gospel of grace moves us to share the word of life with others so that they may experience this heavenly transfer as well.

Another example of the "before and after" shift occurs in 1 Corinthians 2:6–7. Here, Paul talks about the wisdom and rulers of this age. He contrasts this with a knowledge of the gospel that God has revealed to those who no longer dwell in the former age. Those who have not accepted Christ still live in the old age, the old place, and think in these foolish ways, whereas believers have the revelation of Christ and the gospel in their new heavenly dwelling. They view life through the lens of "Christ and him crucified" and live out of the power of the Spirit (1 Cor. 2:2, 4–5). In the new place, the believer gains a new, enhanced gospel lens and knowledge that those dwelling in the old place do not possess.

In a similar manner Paul calls the church of Thessalonica to remain alert to the coming of Christ and to not fall asleep. His justification for their wakefulness resides in their new location: "But you are not in darkness, brothers, for that day to surprise you like a thief. For you are all children of light, children of the day. We are not of the night or of the darkness" (1 Thess. 5:4–5). Light signifies the new heavenly place, while darkness represents the old age and old place. Paul suggests that the person living in the new heavenly place should live with a constant vigilance and awareness of the imminent return of Jesus.

In these admonitions, Paul calls for believers to reorient the way they think and live in relation to their new heavenly location. He repeatedly says, "You don't live in the kingdom of darkness any longer. God the Father has brought you into a new time and new land. Think heavenly. Live like a citizen of the heavenly realm. Be a top-down thinker." That admonition extends to you and me. The apostle pleads with us to think with heaven as the center of our spiritual residence.

So far I have focused a great deal on how the transfer to the new location transforms the way we live. As I mentioned before, certain places can influence our mood as well. We all have "happy places." I mentioned a bakery, a porch, and a stadium as happy places for me. I know you have some that instantly come to mind as well. With the shift to the new heavenly realm comes a permanent and perpetual "happy place" for the believer. We do not have to get in the car or buy a ticket to enjoy it. We can close our eyes, take a deep breath, say a prayer, and joyfully say, "I dwell in the kingdom of God. I am in the new creation. This is where I live." Remembering this place can only comfort and enliven your soul.

Your Heavenward Journey

For some of us our life experiences help us to feel as if we are moving in a heavenward direction. When my son died and went to live in heaven, so much of my heart traveled with him to glory. God came to my little boy and carried him into his heavenly kingdom above, and certainly it feels like a part of me traveled with him. Before his passing, of course, I realized that with each day, I drew closer to glory, but Cam's glorification induced an acute awareness of my ultimate spiritual destination, an overall change of perspective. You may be able to identify with this change of perspective as a result of a heavenward inflection point. After the death of a loved one or a serious diagnosis, you feel heavenward movement in your life like never before. Maybe your weariness and anguish with the pain of this world have made heaven a more prevalent part of your daily consciousness and longings.

Here's the crazy and fascinating reality according to Paul. Yes, in a sense, you are moving toward heaven. However, in another sense, you are just becoming aware of the place you have already dwelled since you placed your faith in Christ. As we noted earlier, upon your conversion God transferred you to a new heavenly place. I am not discounting the reality that we still physically live in the fallen world with all of its trials and pains. But as challenging as it is to grasp, you spiritually dwell in the kingdom of heaven.

You may have had the experience of falling into a deep sleep on a road trip. As you slumbered, the car covered many miles. When you finally woke up, you reoriented yourself to the new surroundings during those first few moments. You looked out the window to get your bearings. You looked for a road sign or for a familiar landmark to ascertain where you were. As you wiped the sleep from your eyes and yawned, you may have asked your parents or your companions, "Where are we?" There had been a major shift in location—many miles had been covered—but to you, it felt instantaneous, which necessitated a process of reorientation.

In some ways, the heavenward journey involves a similar process of reorientation, wherein you awaken to the reality that you are in a new location, the kingdom of heaven. Your physical surroundings in no way help you get your bearings; they are all the same. In the word of God, though, you start to learn the features of this new kingdom. The New Testament, particularly Paul's letters, inform you of the features and realities of your new spiritual place.

While the reorientation in the car may take a few seconds or a minute, this heavenly reorientation transpires over the course of your Christian life. As confusing as this may sound, this process involves awakening to the place you have been ever since Christ saved you.

Unfortunately for many, they never realize that God has transferred them to a new place. They view their heavenly citizenship as something exclusively future rather than present. As a result, they do not experience the transformation of the new location to the fullest. For you, though, Paul makes clear that while you still have a foot in fallen world, you truly live in the kingdom of heaven and in the new creation. Your citizenship is in heaven. When you realize your true, heavenly location, your customs, preferences, and worldview likely will change. The trajectory of your heart and mind certainly will turn upward. Knowing and remembering this place will bring more peace, hope, and joy to your life.

For those suffering, this new location can bring you hope. The scenery of the fallen world can dominate your perspective from day to day and depress you. Watching a nurse put an IV in a loved one's arm for a chemotherapy treatment, peering at tombstones in a cemetery, and watching exchanges of anger and hatred on a Twitter thread can elicit sorrow and despair. While certainly you do have a foot in the fallen world, you have another foot equally planted in the new heavenly place, where the life and love of Christ's redemption abound. Lament the darkness where one foot lies, but do not forget the glorious light under which the other foot dwells.

As it pertains to my child in heaven, remembering my heavenly location reminds me that, in a sense, we both have feet planted on common ground. We cannot see each other. We cannot communicate. Still, we both breathe the same air of the heavenly realm since we both live within the kingdom of heaven—just in different ways.

5

The Communion of Heaven

Union with Christ

MANY WOULD AGREE that the deepest, most painful ailments of life in the fallen world are loneliness and disconnection. Times of suffering and grief often magnify the misery of alienation. Hardly any suffering can surpass the miserable loneliness of feeling as if nobody understands, no one is with you, and the world has passed you by. As total, permanent isolation defines the experience of hell; perfect communion with God and the saints defines the joyful euphoria of heaven. This chapter passes you a cup of the primary thing that can relieve the mutual loneliness that we all experience from the fall and provide the richest taste of heaven on this side of glory. The cup is filled with union with Christ.

In understanding why Paul had such a heavenward mindset, we have established two mammoth factors: Paul believed (1) that heaven had come to earth in the Christ Event and (2) that believers go to dwell in the heavenly realm upon conversion. Our next factor, union with Christ, is one of the most challenging to understand but powerful to enjoy when you comprehend this amazing element of your salvation. Stick with the hard reading in this chapter because these realities will rock your world in a life-giving way.

In 2015 after finishing up an exhausting ministry conference, I treated myself to a book purchase for the plane flight home. This book, *One with Christ* by Marcus Peter Johnson, changed my life.[1] It opened my heart and mind to union with Christ, which Constantine Campbell calls the "webbing" that holds together all of salvation in Paul.[2]

In simple terms, union with Christ involves oneness, connection, and identification with Jesus. In Paul's letters, the prepositions *in*, *with*, and *through*, when used in conjunction with "Christ," "Jesus," "the Lord," or "him," almost always refer to union with Christ. For example, when Paul writes, "Be strengthened by the grace that is *in Christ Jesus*" (2 Tim. 2:1), or, "Be strong *in the Lord*" (Eph. 6:10), he refers to gaining strength via union with Christ. When Paul writes, "I have been crucified *with Christ*," or, "Your life is hidden *with Christ* in God," these statements allude to union with Christ.

In Paul, we observe two facets of this connection to Jesus: past union with Christ and present union with Christ. Richard Gaffin more specifically calls them "redemptive-historic" and "present-experiential" union with Christ.[3]

1 Marcus Peter Johnson, *One with Christ: An Evangelical Theology of Salvation* (Wheaton, IL: Crossway, 2013).

2 Constantine R. Campbell, *Paul and Union with Christ: An Exegetical and Theological Study* (Grand Rapids, MI: Zondervan, 2012), 441.

3 Richard B. Gaffin Jr., *Resurrection and Redemption: A Study in Paul's Soteriology* (Phillipsburg, NJ: P&R, 1978), 49.

Present union with Christ is both mystical and straightforward. When young children declare that they have asked Jesus into their heart, they are accurately describing an element of their salvation that most Christian adults overlook. Upon repentance and faith, Jesus comes into a believer's heart through the Holy Spirit. Simultaneously, in a manner that we cannot comprehend, the believer dwells in the heart of Christ. (Yes, as hard as it is to understand, the union and indwelling go both ways.) Jesus says to his disciples in John 14:20, "In that day you will know that I am in my Father, and *you in me*, and *I in you*." This mutual indwelling creates a life-giving, transformative intimacy in relationship with Jesus.

How close to you is Jesus in times of isolation? He literally dwells in your soul. How close are you to your Savior, Christ, who sits at the right hand of God? Even though he is in heaven, you dwell in his heart too.

In past union with Christ, a believer is unified with Christ in the atoning work of the Christ Event. In every facet of his atoning work and in each redemptive act, we were connected to Jesus. Richard Gaffin characterizes this comprehensive union as "union with Christ in all phases of his messianic work and all that he is by virtue of this work."[4] We were united to Christ in his crucifixion, death, and resurrection (Rom. 6:5; Col. 2:12). And, finally, in this mind-blowing declaration, we were unified with Christ in his ascension. Unification in the ascension of Jesus represents a showstopper in the heavenward journey.

How much does your salvation matter to God? How personal and intimate is the Lord's plan for your redemption? Christ

4 Gaffin, *Resurrection and Redemption*, 45.

literally had you in his heart and mind as he trudged through his atoning life and death.

Both present and past union with Christ have central implications for why Paul was so heavenward. We will start with past union with Christ, as, in this case, the past enables the present.

Unification with Christ in His Ascension

Have you ever wondered how Christ's atoning life, death, and resurrection translate to you, the individual Christian, approximately two thousand years later? Paul answered this question in a mysterious but clear manner. Before your birth, God unified you to Jesus in the events of his atoning mission.

You were connected to Christ in his crucifixion and death. Paul wrote in Galatians 2:20, "I have been *crucified with Christ*. It is no longer I who live." In Romans 6:5 he similarly said, "If we have been united *with him in a death* like his, we shall certainly be united with him in a resurrection like his." Again in Romans 6, Paul used language very similar to that which he used in Galatians 2: "We know that our old self was *crucified with him* in order that the body of sin might be brought to nothing, so that we would no longer be enslaved to sin" (Rom. 6:6). In the moments when Christ died on the cross, God identified you and me as immersed in and unified with Jesus.

Second, God connected us to Christ in his resurrection. In Colossians Paul wrote, "Having been buried with him in baptism, in which you were also *raised with him* through faith in the powerful working of God, who raised him from the dead . . . " (2:12). In the same way that Christ "carried" us through his sacrificial death, the Lord carried us through Jesus's resurrection. As Jesus emerged from the grave, God identified us as unified with him in this redemptive moment.

Obviously, these truths are beyond our comprehension. How were you and I "in Christ" as the Romans nailed his hands to the cross and as he cried out, "My God, my God, why have you forsaken me?" (Matt. 27:46; Mark 15:34)?

How were we unified with Jesus when the stone rolled away and he walked victoriously out of the tomb? While the answers are beyond our comprehension, Scripture clearly demonstrates that, in fact, God united us to Jesus in his death and resurrection (Rom. 6:3–8; Gal. 2:20; Col. 2:12).

Given the way that we experience death and new life in our conversion and Christian life, we may be able to somewhat conceive of our union with Christ in his death and resurrection. But what about his ascension? I cannot say that I have ever heard a sermon or church lesson about our union with Christ in his ascension. Still, Paul mentions our immersion in Christ in his glorious ascension as prevalently as he does the other aspects of the Christ Event. Our connection to Christ in his ascension constitutes one of the most influential factors in Paul's heavenward heart and life.

Prepare yourself for the mystery and awesomeness of these truths. First, in Ephesians 1 Paul describes the redemptive work of Jesus all the way from before the foundation of the world and through the cross and resurrection. The climax of his redemptive victory involved his ascension to the throne of God. After God the Father raised Jesus from the dead, he:

> *seated [Christ] at his right hand in the heavenly places*, far above
> all rule and authority and power and dominion, and above every

name that is named, not only in this age but also in the one to come. And he put all things under his feet and gave him as head over all things to the church. (Eph. 1:20–22)

In Ephesians 1 Paul provides the big-picture summary of Christ's victory, which concludes with Jesus ascending to his position at the right hand of the Father, from which he brings all things under his rule.

In Ephesians 2 the apostle discusses our individual salvation in light of Christ's heavenly rule. He depicts our union with Christ in his ascension in this manner: God "made us alive together with Christ . . . and *raised us up with him* and *seated us with him in the heavenly places in Christ Jesus*" (2:4–6). As God raised Jesus up into heaven, we were in Christ. Upon his arrival there (or should I say *our* arrival), God seated us with Christ and in Christ. Where did we travel? Where were we seated? In the heavenly realms!

Imagine this. As the disciples and others watched Jesus in all of his majesty ascend into heaven forty days after his resurrection, we were in the heart of Jesus on this glorious upward journey. Once we arrived in heaven, God situated us before and in Jesus, where he seated us. To me, this carries hospitable overtones of the Father placing you and me in a fancy, ultracomfortable chair in which we sit and gaze upon the beauty of Jesus and from which we begin to worship him.

Paul reveals in Colossians 3:1 the natural connection between union with Christ in his ascension and a heavenward mindset. He writes, "If then you *have been raised with Christ*, seek the things that are above, where Christ is, seated at the right hand of God." The raising to which Paul refers most likely alludes to our union with him in his ascension. Some people reasonably believe that Paul refers to being raised with Christ in his resurrection here, but the fact that Paul references thinking about "things above" and includes Christ's position "at the right hand of God" suggests that he has union with Christ in his ascension in mind. Therefore, if we ascended with Jesus into heaven, we naturally should have our mind and heart set on heaven. Particularly since, as Christ is seated in heaven, we too are seated in the heavenly realms and unified with him.

Meditating on these truths can change everything in your fellowship with Christ. Watchman Nee built his concept of Christian spirituality around God seating us with Christ in heaven. Nee said:[5]

> The first half of [Ephesians] reveals our life in Christ to be one of union with him in the highest heavens. The second half shows us in very practical terms how much a heavenly life is to be lived by us down here on the earth. . . . God has made us to sit with Christ in the heavenly places, and every Christian must begin his spiritual life from that place of rest. . . . By faith we see ourselves seated together with him in the heavens.[6]

I cannot think of a better way to envision our time in prayer, worship, or Scripture than as one seated before the throne of

---

5   One word of caution I would offer. I would not full-stop endorse all of Watchman Nee's theology. There are some questionable and problematic aspects of his beliefs found in his other writings. One can learn more about this in Dana Roberts's book *Understanding Watchman Nee*. Still, I think Nee captures the spiritual impact and blessing of our unification with Christ in his ascension in a biblically sound and valuable way in the quoted passage.

6   Watchman Nee, *Sit, Stand, Walk* (Carol Stream, IL: Tyndale, 1957), x–xi, 2.

Christ in heaven. While depending on the Holy Spirit, we can conceive of ourselves as sitting in a chair that God himself has prepared for us before the majestic luminescence of the ascended Christ. We sit secure. We rest before his radiant glory. From there, Christ conveys grace to our soul and leads us deeper and deeper into joyful fellowship with him.

Hence, you can see that union with Christ in his ascension does not simply constitute interesting theological trivia, but a foundation of the heavenward life. It guides us in prayer and communion before him and helps us to drink in the richness of fellowship with God.

Present Union with Christ in the Heavenward Life

Occasionally in literature, a writer conveys the truth of a thousand words in a concise phrase. René Descartes declared, *Cogito ergo sum*, which means "I think, therefore I am." The philosopher encapsulated the entirety of his proof of human existence in three short words. Similarly Jesus captured the consummation of his redemptive work on the cross in a compact sentence: "It is finished" (John 19:30). Jesus expressed in that moment that he had completed God's mission for all times on the cross.

Relative to the impact of present union with Christ on the heavenward life, Paul says so much with so little in Colossians 1:27: "Christ in you, the hope of glory." In Greek, hope does not have the flimsy, "maybe, maybe not" connotations of modern English. New Testament hope entails confident expectation. Therefore, in Colossians 1:27 Paul is saying that the current presence of Jesus in your heart provides the certain confidence of your future life in heaven. Present union with Christ comprises one of the richest foretastes of the future heavenly life during our present time in the fallen earth.

Before we can drive that point home, we need to bridge past union with Christ to present union with Christ and demonstrate how they interrelate.[7] Paul demonstrates this relationship clearly in Galatians 2:20: "I *have been crucified with Christ*. It is no longer I who live, but *Christ who lives in me*. And the life I now live in the flesh I live by faith in the Son of God, who loved me and gave himself for me." Paul links his past union with Christ in his crucifixion to his present union with Christ. On the cross, Jesus remediates the problem of sin, which stood as the barrier between a believer and present communion with God.

At what point does a person cross the threshold of having been unified with Christ in the past to now experiencing union in the present? When the Holy Spirit regenerates a believer's soul from death to new life and the believer repents and believes in Christ, past union and present union converge.

In Colossians 2:13 and Ephesians 2:5 Paul uses a unique expression, "made alive together with Christ" or "made alive with him," that signifies that precise moment of conversion. J. B. Lightfoot translates this phrase to mean that the Christian is "resurrected in experience to the resurrection life."[8] Here is where Gaffin's term "present-experiential" union with Christ is valuable. After God has made us "alive together with Christ," we *experience* the

---

7 John Murray writes: "Union with Christ is a very inclusive subject. It embraces the wide span of salvation from its ultimate source in the eternal election of God to its final fruition in the glorification of the elect." John Murray, *Redemption Accomplished and Applied* (Grand Rapids, MI: Eerdmans, 2015), 172–75.

8 J. B. Lightfoot, *Saint Paul's Epistles to the Colossians and to Philemon* (Grand Rapids, MI: Zondervan, 1974), n.p.

resurrection life of the new heavenly realm through our present union with Christ. We *experience* the fruit of Jesus's work to bring us into the joy and renewal of the heavenly realms.

Max Turner reinforces the present, eschatological significance of being "made alive together with Christ" in this passage:

> To say we have been made alive with Christ appears to be shorthand for saying, "we shall be resurrected with Christ to new-creation life," and we may speak of that as though it were an already-accomplished event because, first, the decisive event of the resurrection of the representative Man Jesus lies in the past and secondly, we already begin to participate in aspects of that new-creation life *in our present union with him.*[9]

In other words, our union with Jesus in the Christ Event leads to our conversion by faith. Our conversion by faith leads us to experience the joy of the heavenly life, which is defined by union with Christ.

Again, present union with Christ defines the experience of the heavenly life that we enjoy as we walk with Jesus. Paul wrote in 2 Corinthians 5:17, "If anyone is in Christ, he is a new creation." We tend to interpret this verse on the surface as, "If I am in relationship with Christ, I am a new person." This translation has merit. However, the more central essence of the verse means that a person who is in union with Christ lives in the new creation and, while still a sinner, enjoys the spiritual life of the new heavenly

---

9 Max Turner, "Ephesians," in *New Bible Commentary: 21st Century Edition*, ed. Gordon Wenham, J. A. Motyer, and D. A. Carson et al. (Downers Grove, IL: InterVarsity Press, 1994), 1229; emphasis original.

age. As a result of this, he has been resurrected to "newness of life," as Paul said in Romans 6. The newness of life involves the joy, hope, and vitality of present heavenly life, which we experience as we enjoy our union with Christ.

A clear intermingling and interrelatedness exist between experiencing union with Christ and enjoying the heavenly life. We see this both in Scripture and in the writings of church history. In her classic mystical itinerary *The Interior Castle*, Teresa of Ávila wrote about cultivating intimacy with Jesus through the extended metaphor of a person walking deeper and deeper into the interior of a castle. The castle itself represents living within the heavenly, spiritual realm. The journey within the castle (which again represents the spiritual realm) involves movement in experiencing greater intimacy with Jesus, which Teresa grounds in union with Christ. In one part, she describes our fellowship with God in this way: "This secret union takes place in the deepest centre of the soul, which must be where God Himself dwells."[10] While instructing people how to draw deeper into the present heavenly life, she emphasizes the mutual indwelling of us in Christ and Christ in us. The present, eternal joys of the heavenward life and participation in union with Christ go hand in hand.

British poet George Herbert demonstrated similar intermingling of union with Christ and the present heavenly life in his poem "Colossians 3:3":

My words and thoughts do both express this notion,
That Life hath with the sun a double motion.

10 Teresa of Ávila, *The Interior Castle* (New York: Image, 2013), n.p.

The first Is straight, and our diurnal friend,
The other Hid, and doth obliquely bend.
One life is wrapped In flesh, & and tends to earth:
The other winds towards Him, whose happy birth
Taught me to live here so, That still one eye
Should aim and shoot at that which Is on high:
Quitting with daily labour all My pleasure,
To gain at harvest an eternal Treasure.

The spiritual life involves being "Hid" in Christ, referring to our dwelling in him. To project life in an upward, eternal trajectory means to live into the reality of our union with Jesus. Petr Pokorný, commenting on Colossians 3:3, sums it up well: "The only thing which characterizes the new life (both on earth and in heaven) is fellowship with Jesus Christ."[11]

The intimate fellowship with Jesus that comes through union with Christ constitutes the single richest taste of heaven on earth. Next to our vision of God in his glory, the other defining feature of heaven will be full communion with Jesus. We had union with Christ in his past atoning work. We will experience perfect union with Christ when we live in heaven. Today, believer, you have union with Christ. Drink in the heavenly by drawing near to Jesus.

Your Heavenward Journey

As I've said before, the deepest grief I experience in the loss of my child is the separation from Cam. Most of the things we attempt to do in grief involve trying to generate some sort of connection.

---

11 Petr Pokorný, *Colossians: A Commentary* (Peabody, MA: Hendrickson, 1991), 160.

When I drive by the old house where we raised him and glance at the window to his room, out of which he would peek during naps, and when I look at old pictures, tell past stories, or watch old videos, I am trying to create some sense of connection with my little boy.

Cherishing these memories creates a simple little bridge to him of sorts. These practices are good things. In a sense, these practices function as if I am drawing heaven—where he lives—a little closer to me. However, what about connecting with him by drawing myself closer to heaven?

Union with Christ constitutes one of the fundamental pillars of heaven. In heaven, a central aspect of our joy and euphoria will be the intimacy we enjoy with God. We will realize and savor our oneness with the Lord. With that being said, we are presently one with God through union with Christ. Certainly, because of sin and the challenges of the fallen world, we do not taste this communion now as we will then. But that doesn't mean that we cannot sample the heavenly banquet here and now. Pursuing intimacy with Jesus in our daily lives is to elevate more and more into the heavenly airs of life in Christ.

In turn, "rising up" into heavenly airs by drawing closer to Christ creates a closer sense of connection with our loved ones above too. This enjoyment of our union with Christ assuages the isolation that is inherent to life in the fallen world and which is particularly pronounced in a season of grief. It soothes the sense of disconnection we feel with our lost loved ones. It soothes the common isolation that can plague our lives on earth.

If I want to feel close to Cam, the best thing I can do is draw close to Jesus.

6

The Vision of Heaven

Seeing Christ

MANY MARRIED MEN can agree on the single most glorious sight and exhilarating moment of their lives—their wedding day when they saw their bride come down the aisle. There, the radiant beauty of their wife and the fulfillment of so many desires intersected. Similarly, many parents would identify the birth of their child as the pinnacle of their time on earth. Though the baby may have been covered in blood and fluid and crying stridently, most parents would say they had never seen anything so beautiful nor felt so much love and joy in their hearts. In both cases, a sight constitutes a pinnacle of life. More specifically, the sight of a person—a particular person—is the mountain top.

For the Christian, the climax of all existence, the satisfaction of all longings, the moment to which all glorious moments points, is the face-to-face vision of Jesus upon entry into heaven. All people at various times have succumbed to the false notion that there will be a day on earth when they will be satisfied. Perhaps you've looked forward to a wedding day, to having kids, to a possession, to a season of physical health, to crossing a financial threshold, or to retirement. Beyond the horizon of all those potentially blessed moments lies the ultimate threshold: the face of Jesus Christ and the vision thereof.

Randy Alcorn in his classic book *Heaven* wrote, "In heaven, the barriers between redeemed human beings and God will forever be gone. To look into God's eyes will be to see what we've always longed to see: the person who made us for his own good pleasure."[1]

Irenaeus rightly said, "The end of life is the vision of God."[2] Scripture validates this statement. When God provides a vivid glimpse into the experience of the new heaven and new earth in Revelation, the vision of God stands at the center. There will be the elimination of pain and suffering, there will be the luminescence of Christ, and there will be the worship of God. All of this worship and radiance flow out of the reality that "they will see his face" (Rev. 22:4).

Paul wrote in 1 Corinthians 13:12, "For now we see in a mirror dimly, but then face to face." He defines the incomplete and partial nature of the Christian life on earth as seeing God only in part. He defines the nature of the consummated life of glory as seeing Christ face-to-face. John reinforced this notion in 1 John 3, where he wrote, "We are God's children now, and what we will be

---

1   Randy Alcorn, *Heaven: A Comprehensive Guide to Everything the Bible Says about Our Eternal Home (Clear Answers to 44 Real Questions about the Afterlife, Angels, Resurrection, and the Kingdom of God)* (Carol Stream, IL: Tyndale, 2004), 175.

2   Kenneth Kirk translated or adapted a quote of Iranaeus's in this way in Kenneth E. Kirk, *The Vision of God* (Cambridge, UK: James Clarke, 1977).

has not yet appeared; but we know that when he appears we shall be like him, because we shall see him as he is" (v. 2). John admits that we do not know exactly what we will be like in heaven, but we do know that when Christ appears, we will be transformed purely by the sight of him.

For Paul, seeing the glorified Christ, which is often referred to as the "beatific vision," served as the bookends of his life. Therefore, the beatific vision was central to his heavenward life, and it can be central to ours too.

The Vision of Christ, the Bookends of Paul's Spiritual Life

We've already seen how Paul's entire life and ministry radically changed when he encountered Jesus on the road to Damascus, as recorded in Acts 9. In a previous chapter, I explained how this moment awakened Paul to the redemptive historic implications of the Christ Event relative to the day of the Lord and the age to come. However, I did not assert just how instrumental this moment was to Paul's heavenward spirituality.

Author and professor Greg Lanier has made a comparison between Paul's vision of Christ on the Damascus road and the theophanies of the prophets Moses (Ex. 3), Isaiah (Isa. 6), Daniel (Dan. 10), and Ezekiel (Ezek. 1–2) in the Old Testament.[3] (A theophany refers to a visible manifestation of God to humankind.) At the pivotal moments at the beginnings of the ministries of these prophets, God appeared to them. They saw the Lord in some powerful, over-the-top, supernatural fashion.

---

3   Lanier taught this in lectures about the Pauline epistles at Reformed Theological Seminary. They can be accessed at https://rts.edu/resource_types/lectures/.

Lanier identifies common themes among these Old Testament theophanies that align with Paul's encounter with Jesus. The sight came unexpectedly with radiant light and a heavenly vision. The prophet fell to the ground as a divine voice directly addressed them and commissioned them to preach to God's people through the Holy Spirit. These theophanies fueled their ministries.

Paul's theophany was no different. Unexpectedly, "a light from heaven shone around him" (Acts 9:3). He fell to the ground and heard the voice of God addressing him, questioning his persecution of Christians and then giving him directions. Then, through words given to Ananias, the Lord commissioned Paul as "a chosen instrument of mine to carry my name before the Gentiles and kings and the children of Israel" (9:15).

Out of this moment, Paul flew forward as a supernova of the gospel, the world's greatest theologian, and a prolific church planter. He lived with an undeterred hope and belief. And it all came back to his vision of God in the glorified Christ. One can assume that seeing God fueled Paul's life and ministry and was the center of his future expectation. When Paul thought of heaven, his primary excitement most likely centered on seeing the heavenly Christ face-to-face—once again.

For many of us, the beatific vision has played either a small or nonexistent role in our conception of heaven. Michael Allen's book *Grounded in Heaven* largely critiques the absence of the beatific vision in twentieth- and twenty-first-century theologies of heaven.[4] Theologians and pastors have dedicated primary attention to the physical nature of the new heaven and new earth

---

4   Michael Allen, *Grounded in Heaven: Recentering Christian Hope and Life on God* (Grand Rapids, MI: Eerdmans, 2018).

and little attention to the sight of God. Let's be honest: many Christians are more curious about whether or not their dog will be in heaven than seeing the face of Jesus there.

The neglect of the beatific vision creates a significant problem in the heavenward journey because it decentralizes the center of heaven, Jesus himself. Secondary benefits of heaven become primary, and the primary becomes dethroned. As I've often said, what makes heaven *heaven* is the full presence *and sight* of Jesus. However, when the vision of God becomes fundamental in our heavenly consciousness, our hearts and minds are set in the right place: on Jesus. They are set on the source of strength and joy that actually carries us home and unto the other side. John Owen once wrote, "Think much of him who unto us is the life and center of all the glory of heaven; that is, Christ himself."[5]

Indeed, conceiving of heaven with the vision of Christ at the center purifies our spiritual lives. It directs our longings more toward God and less toward our idols. Thus, with our eyes fixed on the vision of God as our future hope, living heavenward involves a life more centered on the Lord.

The Sight of God in Day-to-Day Life

The fourth-century mystic Gregory of Nyssa wrote about the life of Moses as a spiritual itinerary whereby Moses first saw God in the burning bush and then again on Mount Sinai. Moses's vision of God created the arc of his life. He first saw God and began to follow him. His vision of God's glory guided and sustained him at critical moments. And his life continued on toward the

5   John Owen, *Sin and Grace*, vol. 7, *The Works of John Owen* (London: Banner of Truth, 1965), 334.

ultimate vision of God in eternity. Pursuing God meant pursuing the vision of God here and now.

This reality may be true for people like Moses, Isaiah, Daniel, Ezekiel, and Paul in unique circumstances, but theophanies of this sort do not ordinarily occur. You may have heard stories of people in the missions frontier having dreams and visions where they saw Jesus and then heard the gospel, but, by and large, most of us have never met a person who's had a theophanic experience. We don't build our lives on the expectation that Jesus will appear to us during worship service or during a walk down the street, while waiting in the checkout line at the grocery store or while sitting in the carpool line.

Nevertheless, Paul does say in 1 Corinthians 13:12, "*For now we see* in a mirror *dimly.*" It is important to note that mirrors in the ancient world were polished metal that provided opaque images. A person could see a semblance of their reflection but nothing close to the real thing. We do not fully see God in the way we will in heaven. Still, Paul did say that, in a partial manner, we can see Christ dimly.

In 2 Corinthians 3:18 Paul wrote, "We all, with unveiled face, beholding the glory of the Lord, are being transformed into the same image from one degree of glory to another. For this comes from the Lord who is the Spirit." Through the coming of Christ and the indwelling of the Holy Spirit, God has lifted the former veil from our face to enable us to see his glory. Though not in full, the Holy Spirit partially helps us to see God's heavenly glory.

The primary ways in which we gain the partial vision of Christ in this life come through God's word and through the empowerment of the Holy Spirit. All of God's word reveals an image of the Lord. Even more specifically, through apocalyptic scriptures such as those in Ezekiel, Isaiah, Daniel, and Revelation, the Lord provides symbolic pictures of God in heaven and of his glorious works. Many psalms depict the Lord sitting upon a throne of righteousness. Through the language and images in Scripture, the Spirit enables us to see God, however dim and partial the sight may be. At a deeper level, however, we see the Lord as his character, beauty, and attributes shine through the words of Scripture. We gain a vision of the glory of God in every passage of the Bible as the Holy Spirit gives us a picture of who God is. In prayer, while depending on the Holy Spirit, we can meditate on the images of Scripture and ask the Lord to bless us with a modest glimpse of his heavenly glory.

Furthermore, God has revealed his divine attributes through the beauty of creation. Paul wrote in Romans 1:20, "For his invisible attributes, namely, his eternal power and divine nature, have been clearly perceived, ever since the creation of the world, in the things that have been made." We see God's eternal majesty in the beautiful scenes in nature. That beauty will be magnified infinitely when God's presence fills the earth in the new heaven and new earth. In moments when we are blessed to see the beauty of mountains, rivers, oceans, plains, lakes, valleys, creeks, flowers, and trees, through prayerful meditation we can enjoy a partial sight of God's future glory on the earth.

Knowing that our heart's deepest longing points to seeing Jesus, we can move heavenward by seeking the vision of God day by day in our spiritual lives. We pursue this partial sight of God through prayer and meditation on the images of Christ and God's glory, which Scripture provides. With the help of the Holy Spirit, we look upon the beauty of God's creation and imagine how the Lord will heighten these majestic scenes when he returns. In this way, heavenward spirituality involves using God's means of revelation to gain a less dim and less partial vision of Christ and his glory.

All Questions Answered

One of the enduring pains of this life involves living with the agonizing *whys*—the questions that often torment us with no resolution. My wife and I know many couples who have lost children, and we have heard many awful stories. One story in particular has always gnawed at my soul. The couple struggled with infertility for years and years. After years of disappointment, they decided to adopt, and they received a wonderful daughter. They had come to peace with the permanence of infertility and embraced the joy of raising their adopted daughter. Then their miracle came. The wife became pregnant. Their exuberance was so great that she said that she rejoiced in morning sickness. Out of nowhere, apart from all expectations, she was living her dream!

And then it happened. In the second trimester, the mother sensed that something had gone awry in the pregnancy, so she went to the doctor. Indeed, a nightmare was upon them. The baby had died. The mother delivered the deceased child, and the family entered into not only the grief of losing a baby, but also the lament and confusion of an inexplicable chapter of their lives.

The wife said that as reverent as she wanted to be, the loss felt like a "sucker punch from God." They had grieved the cutting disappointment of infertility and faithfully moved forward. They had their dream dangled right in front of their eyes and in their hearts, only to have it all shattered. There was no nonprofit established, no book written, no future pregnancy later. Absolutely no silver lining. At all.

Too often Christians with good intentions but with unwise execution rush to put a silver lining on tragedy. *Because your son died, this really good thing came out of it. See, that makes it all better, right?* Tragedies and traumas inevitably occur in life for which any attempted silver-lining explanation can only end in insult. There are pains we carry our entire lives for which God never supplies any kind of suitable revelation of his purposes.

Why did my friend's otherwise healthy dad drop dead thirty-six hours before his wedding? Why did that person who heard the gospel continually and for whom dozens of people prayed reject Christ all the way into eternity? Why did the driver cross the median in that moment and on that night? Why did that wicked person choose you or your loved one to assault? Just this sampling of questions likely stirs up pain and anger and outrage in all of us.

Maybe we witness some good arise from these excruciating questions, but we will all carry unresolved, deeply aggravating questions to our graves.

The vision of God in heaven does offer resolution to this trial of the fallen life. In the second half of 1 Corinthians 13:12, Paul wrote, "Now I know in part; then I shall know fully, even as I have been fully known." For now, we have only partial revelation about God. The revelation we have in the Bible is completely sufficient for salvation, godliness, teaching, and correction, but until we see Jesus face-to-face, what we know about God and his purposes is partial (2 Tim. 3:16–17). However, then—when we see Jesus face-to-face—we shall *know fully*, as we are currently fully understood by God in this struggle.

And let me tell you how I think this will happen. As you carry those questions in your pocket into glory, there will not be a sit-down conversation with Christ in which you ask, "Jesus, why did I have that miscarriage? Why did that awful thing happen to me?" and Christ offers you an explanation so you can then say, "Oh, that makes sense. I get it now."

No, you will see Jesus in all of his glorious splendor, and in that moment, in that blink of an eye, every single question will be resolved. An explanation isn't what will satisfy you and me; the sight of the infinite, magnificent, transparent goodness, beauty, and supremacy of the Lord God himself will settle all accounts and answer all questions. Because when you see Christ face-to-face with no veil to lift and no partiality, his goodness and beauty alone will satisfy every single question.

Your Heavenward Journey

Many of you can relate to how I think every day about seeing my son in heaven. I anticipate and long for the moment when I enter into glory, and he comes running for me, and we embrace, and I say, "Finally!" It probably stands as the single moment I anticipate the most.

As much as I envision seeing Cam first upon my entrance to heaven, in reality, no matter how much I love Cam and how glorious the sight of him may be, my eyes will be fixed on Christ. All beauty, all majesty, all glory in all the universe emanate from the face of Jesus.

I'd imagine that the moments will play out more in this way. As I pass through the heavenly gates my eyes will marvel at the majesty of Christ. I will go to my knees with tears in my eyes, beholding the face of Jesus. And I will feel a hand embrace mine, and perhaps hear a voice saying, "Isn't He wonderful, Dad?" Then I will feel the hands of my father and grandparents on my shoulders as they too continue to gaze upon and worship and stare at the beautiful Christ. And as long as I have waited to see them all, particularly my child, I am not sure that I'll be able to take my eyes off Jesus.

Of course, none of us knows exactly how this will transpire, but I do know that nothing can or will outshine the sight of God in heaven. So let us live the heavenward life by seeking the face of God in his word and creation with the power of the Holy Spirit, and by anticipating the glorious sight of him.

7

The Power of Heaven

The Holy Spirit

AS A BOY, I DESPERATELY wanted a dog. For three years I asked for the gift of a puppy at Christmas, on my birthday, and at any other pertinent occasion. Finally, in a moment of weakness while on vacation, my dad gave in to my persistence. *Hallelujah!* I was elated!

We soon bought a Welsh springer spaniel, a somewhat rare breed. Since Welsh springers were hard to find, we had to purchase the dog prior to its birth and then wait several months for my puppy, Towy. When I saw that sweet little face peering through the dog kennel for the first time, I was overjoyed, and the experience of having my own dog did not disappoint. Towy brought me so much joy throughout my adolescence and early adult life. My dog was everything I dreamed of. As trite as this story may seem, at the age of twelve I had never wanted something so much in my entire life, and then it was fulfilled.

On a much grander scale, God promised in the Old Testament a gift for the age to come, a promise that would create rich, lively expectation for any Jewish reader. It was perhaps the feature of the new heavenly age for which the Jews longed most. When you read these passages, it will create excitement in you as well.

Twice Paul referred to the "promised" Holy Spirit in his letters.[1] Paul did not offer further explanation in relation to this promised gift because God communicated such salient, glorious expectations in the Hebrew scriptures that Jewish readers would presumably know the significant gift to which he referred.

When we integrate all the Holy Spirit promises in the prophets of the Old Testament, a vivid narrative is revealed, which helps us appreciate the powerful heavenly implications of the coming of the Spirit. First, Isaiah paints the picture of a messianic King who will rule "in righteousness" over a total restoration of the fallen world. However, the King will not initiate this renewal of creation "until the Spirit is poured upon us from on high" (Isa. 32:15). Then, through the Holy Spirit:

> The wilderness becomes a fruitful field,
>   and the fruitful field is deemed a forest.
> Then justice will dwell in the wilderness,
>   and righteousness abide in the fruitful field.
> And the effect of righteousness will be peace,
>   and the result of righteousness, quietness and trust forever.

---

1   "In him you also, when you heard the word of truth, the gospel of your salvation, and believed in him, were sealed with the promised Holy Spirit" (Eph. 1:13); "So that in Christ Jesus the blessing of Abraham might come to the Gentiles, so that we might receive the promised Spirit through faith" (Gal. 3:14).

My people will abide in a peaceful habitation,
in secure dwellings, and in quiet resting places.
And it will hail when the forest falls down,
and the city will be utterly laid low.
Happy are you who sow beside all waters,
who let the feet of the ox and the donkey range free.
(32:15–20)

Through the activity of the Holy Spirit, the messianic King ushers in an era of healing, peace, justice, and happiness. The messianic King oversees and the Spirit creates a heavenly age on the earth. In multiple places, Isaiah reinforces this vision of messianic renewal through the Holy Spirit.[2]

Ezekiel also portrays a vision of God reviving the entire fallen world through the Holy Spirit. In Ezekiel 37, the prophet described an image of dry bones in a valley taking on flesh and coming alive through the Holy Spirit. Ezekiel proclaims the word of God, which leads to the dry bones taking on flesh. Then in a prophetic image that resembles God breathing life into Adam in Genesis 2, the Lord's breath makes the risen bodies alive. In harkening back to Genesis, Ezekiel expresses a vision of a new creation, with fallen humanity being revived by the word and Spirit of God.[3] The restoration of this vision occurs throughout the entire earth, but it occurs from the ground up. The restoration of individuals through the Spirit precedes and produces the comprehensive, global renewal.

2   These texts about the Messiah renewing the world through the Spirit can be seen clearly in Isa. 42, 44, and 61.
3   John W. Yates, *The Spirit and Creation in Paul*, Wissenschaftliche Untersuchungen zum Neuen Testament 2, Reihe 251 (Tübingen, Germany: Mohr Seibeck, 2008), n.p.

The preceding chapter, Ezekiel 36, highlights this reality of global restoration coming from the regeneration of individuals. God promises:

> I will give you a new heart, and a new spirit I will put within you. And I will remove the heart of stone from your flesh and give you a heart of flesh. And I will put my Spirit within you, and cause you to walk in my statutes and be careful to obey my rules. (36:26–27)

At the base level, God brings about the new life, peace, and justice of the new heavenly age through the transformation of people's hearts. The Holy Spirit indwells the hearts of God's people to enable them to live moral, loving lives, which, in turn, change the whole world.

Hence, the promise of the Holy Spirit in the age to come takes on both grand and simple implications. Joel reinforces this reality when he prophesies that God will "pour out" his Holy Spirit on the day of the Lord (Joel 2:28–29). This pouring out carries connotations of flooding the whole world with the presence of the Spirit. And, at the end of the day, the Spirit falls on all of God's people—male and female, old and young, slave and free. God brings about a new, restored creation, not through a flash of lightning but through restoring individual hearts by the indwelling of the Spirit.

With these Old Testament expectations in mind, Paul explains how the Holy Spirit serves a (if not *the*) central role in the heavenward life of the believer here and now.

The Promised Spirit Realized

So far, many of the foundations of the heavenward life have been "big picture" and grand to the point of seeming out of touch with the person simply hoping to live and walk in a heavenward manner or hoping to find hope in the promises of eternity. The promised Holy Spirit is the key to bringing heavenwardness down to practical, everyday life. That's exactly what Paul does in his letters. He demonstrates how the magnificent realities of this long-awaited gift provide the fuel for the heavenward life for regular people living mundane lives.

Throughout his letters, Paul explains how the Spirit functions as the initiator and sustainer of the new heavenly age. In 1 Corinthians 15:45–49 he states:

> Thus it is written, "The first man Adam became a living being"; the last Adam became a life-giving spirit. But it is not the spiritual that is first but the natural, and then the spiritual. The first man was from the earth, a man of dust; the second man is from heaven. As was the man of dust, so also are those who are of the dust, and as is the man of heaven, so also are those who are of heaven. Just as we have borne the image of the man of dust, we shall also bear the image of the man of heaven.

Paul is setting up a parallel between the old creation in Adam and the new creation in Christ, the second Adam. In 1 Corinthians 15:45 Paul cites Genesis 2:7, where God brought Adam to life through his breath. As God brought life to Adam through his breath, he brings new life to the slain Jesus through his Holy Spirit. As a "natural" or physical life came to Adam through the breath of God, a resurrected life comes to Jesus via the Spirit. As God completed the creation of the physical world by making Adam through his breath, he initiates the new creation by bringing Jesus to life from the grave through his Holy Spirit. This same dynamic involved in the Spirit's activity in raising Jesus applies to every converted believer.

Thus, when you came to faith in Christ, the promised Spirit of the new heavenly age has brought you from death to life. Through this regenerative work, God has brought you into the new heavenly age. It ultimately consummates in the resurrection of the body at the second coming.

In between the spiritual resurrection of initial conversion and the ultimate bodily resurrection, what sustains this heavenward existence? Paul explains in 2 Corinthians 3 that the Holy Spirit sustains and nurtures the heavenward life. In talking about the power of new-covenant ministry and the life of the new creation, the apostle identifies the Holy Spirit as the center of both. Twice in this passage, he associates the Lord and the Spirit. He writes, "Now the Lord is the Spirit, and where the Spirit of the Lord is, there is freedom" (2 Cor. 3:17) and "this comes from the Lord who is the Spirit" (3:18). So much meaning in so few words.

His reference to God as Lord conveys his total rule over the new creation. One can see the images of the messianic King ruling in righteousness over this new heavenly age. Simultaneously, the Holy Spirit carries out this work of renewal; he is the active life force. And where that thriving Spirit dwells and works, there is freedom from the death of the old fallen age.

Again, this big-picture portrayal of global restoration has its foundation in the sanctification of individual hearts. In

2 Corinthians 3:3 Paul writes, "You show that you are a letter from Christ delivered by us, written not with ink but with the Spirit of the living God, not on tablets of stone but on tablets of human hearts." The reference to the Holy Spirit dwelling in and writing on human hearts hearkens back to the prophecies of Ezekiel, where God promises to place his Spirit within his people. From the inside out, God transforms his people and, thereby, transforms the world.

From this basis, the Holy Spirit enables us to see the glory of Jesus in the gospel (2 Cor. 3:16). Through this vibrant work of the Spirit, we "with unveiled face, beholding the glory of the Lord, are being transformed into the same image from one degree of glory to another" (3:18). This change in image describes a moral and spiritual transformation in our lives as we are shaped into people who live more like Christ. While we continue to sin and struggle, this transformation carries us from "one degree of glory to another," meaning that we deepen more and more into the life and experience of the new heavenly age here and now.

Your heart and my heart are ground zero for God's rejuvenation of the world. The Holy Spirit is drawing and pushing us deeper and deeper into the heavenward life. This sanctifying life does involve the discomfort of conviction, contrition, and repentance. The most rancid taste of the old age that we experience is our own sin. The regret and emptiness of being self-absorbed, of wronging others, of overindulging, gossiping, and lusting, leave us with the present evil age's flavor of death in our mouths. The Holy Spirit is God's gift to empower us to repent and walk away from these things and to rinse out this taste. It also provides us with the experience of joy, peace, and gratification when we walk in the ways of the Spirit as earthly people who are more like our heavenly selves.

Again, who effectuates this remarkable metamorphosis? Paul plainly states: "This comes from the Lord who is the Spirit" (3:18). It is the promised Holy Spirit, the heavenly gift of the heavenward life, that makes this all happen.

The Guarantee

So far I have dedicated most of our attention to the present activity of the Holy Spirit in bringing us into the heavenward life. However, Paul several times speaks about the Spirit's function to provide present assurance of future heavenly blessings.

Paul thrice refers to the Holy Spirit as a "down payment" or "guarantee" (2 Cor. 1:22; 5:5; Eph. 1:14). In Ephesians 1:14 he calls it "the *guarantee* of our inheritance until we acquire possession of it." In speaking about our future bodily resurrection at the second coming, the apostle wrote, "He who has prepared us for this very thing [our bodily resurrection] is God, who has given us the Spirit as a *guarantee*" (2 Cor. 5:5). He also states, "It is God who establishes us with you in Christ, and has anointed us, and who has also put his seal on us and given us his Spirit in our hearts as a *guarantee*" (2 Cor. 1:21–22).

We must understand the definition of this guarantee. In the ancient world, when two parties agreed to a large purchase, the buyer would make a down payment to certify the full payment in the future. Today, many people refer to this as "earnest money." The same Greek word used for a down payment is also used in modern Greek for an engagement ring.[4] The ring signifies something far greater down the road. God's gift of the Holy Spirit

---

4 Francis Foulkes, *Ephesians: An Introduction and Commentary*, vol. 10, Tyndale New Testament Commentaries (Downers Grove, IL: InterVarsity Press, 1989), 65.

points to and guarantees two much greater blessings in glory than anything we will taste in this life.

First, in 2 Corinthians 1 Paul states that God has established us "in Christ," which refers to our union with Christ. The indwelling of the Holy Spirit is a partial payment of the full experience of our perfect union with Christ in heaven! If you've ever eaten a small sample at an ice cream shop in one of those tiny little spoons (I am talking about the ones that are smaller than a baby spoon), this minuscule sample illustrates the down payment of the Spirit in this sense. In those moments when you have felt the joy and peace of God's presence at a worship service or a conference or on a mountain hike or when sitting in a hospital bed praying for God's mercy, the Holy Spirit provided that sensation. Even the most spiritually joyful, exuberant moment of your life (however that may have looked for you) was just a tiny little sample of the glorious blessedness of your union with Christ in heaven.

Second, in 2 Corinthians 5 and in Romans 8, Paul identifies the indwelling Spirit as a guarantee of our bodily resurrection. In Romans, he writes that the same Spirit that raised Jesus from the dead "will also give life to your mortal bodies through his Spirit who dwells in you" (8:11). This future giving of life to our bodies refers to our bodily resurrection at the second coming of Christ. In the modest moments when God delivered you from temptation, healed your heart, or led you into loving service, that was the Holy Spirit working redemption in your life. He was bringing life out of death, the very thing that he will do to your mortal body at the second coming of Christ.

Understanding the guarantee of the Holy Spirit is critical for having heavenward hopefulness, because, if you are like me, life usually does not feel very heavenly. I constantly fall back into the same sins. Same temper tantrums, same sharp tongue, same self-absorption. I often feel depressed or anxious or overwhelmed. In spite of all these promises of heaven that we've discussed, this life surely doesn't feel like heaven very often.

And, of course, it doesn't feel like heaven because we are not there yet. We still live in sinful flesh in the fallen world. Lest we fall into despair and write off our heavenly inheritance, the Holy Spirit gives us tiny samples of glory as evidence of our future inheritance. Those modest moments of joy or deliverance or sanctification are very limited assurances that God's heavenly promises are real, true, and reliable. In those experiences where you actually *feel* a tiny sample of glory, God is putting a ring on your finger and saying, "See, I have something so much better in store for you. I promise."

Your Heavenward Journey

So far, I have spent a great deal of time explaining theological truths that can open our eyes to the heavenly realities of our lives. Education can lead to new awakenings and glorious transformation. Still, with all of this new knowledge, the practical question remains: How do I live into this? How does this actually translate into a heavenward life?

Moving into the heavenward life lies on the shoulders of the Holy Spirit, not on you. We cannot make ourselves believe biblical truths. We cannot force our minds to envision ourselves as citizens of heaven, having been transferred into God's heavenly kingdom. We cannot manufacture a vision of Jesus. We cannot maintain a frequent consciousness of the fragility of our lives and our nearness to death.

In our everyday, mundane lives of work and bills and cleaning and family, in our sinful struggles of impulse and relapse and reaction, in our painful lament of depression and disappointment and heartbreak and anxiety, in the irritation and exhaustion and agony of physical ailments—in all these things the momentum of the flesh frequently carries us back into the death and darkness of the fall, which makes the joy and hope of heaven feel utterly distant and faint. Only the Holy Spirit can carry us into the blessedness of the heavenward life. Only the Holy Spirit can bring to life the healing, joy, and light of the present heavenly age.

And the Holy Spirit does just that for you and for me.

In the next section, we will discuss the fruit of the heavenward life. The Holy Spirit, by his grace, bridges the gap between vital knowledge of heavenly realities in your life and actual transformation. It translates the educated mind to the glory-bound heart. The Spirit that raised Jesus from the dead and took him into glory dwells in you and can also take you and me more deeply into the present joy and future hope of the heavenward life.

Ask and trust him to do so. Rely on the Spirit of God.

THE FRUIT OF A HEAVENWARD LIFE

8

The Fruit of Heavenward

Contentment

IF YOU'VE ENGAGED with advertising or popular culture in the twenty-first century, you're most likely familiar with these two slogans: YOLO and FOMO. If you need a refresher, YOLO stands for "You only live once," while FOMO is the "fear of missing out."

Depending on your disposition, you may either pump your fist with enthusiasm or roll your eyes at these two trite slogans. Their overuse has solidified their place in the American vernacular. While these expressions carry lighthearted, nonserious connotations, they do capture a core belief underlying modern culture and a source of much human dissatisfaction.

Think a little more deeply and consider the words as you slowly break them down. YOLO: You. Only. Live. Once. In other words, this life on earth is it. There is nothing at all after death. There is no heaven. You only have this life on earth to enjoy, and upon death your existence ceases. Therefore, live it up here and now!

With this in mind, it makes sense that people often associate YOLO with FOMO. If this life constitutes the entirety of your existence, then you absolutely must maximize your enjoyment. You must never miss an opportunity for fun and pleasure. If this life is it, then you live with a sense of urgency and fear that if you decline an invitation or miss a good time, then you are wasting your one and only finite life.

How do you live your life if, in fact, you only live once, a short life in this fallen world?

This question is nothing new. Our modern YOLO and FOMO are terms for what the ancient Greek and Roman societies knew as Epicureanism. Ancient Greek philosopher Epicurus believed that the world consisted of atoms and basically no more. As a result, he rejected belief in an afterlife. He wrote in his letter to Menoeceus: "Death, therefore, the most awful of evils, is nothing to us, seeing that, when we are, death is not come, and, when death is come, we are not." Indeed, Epicurus believed you only live once.

While Epicurus did not advocate excessive hedonism, his champions applied his worldview and determined that life should involve the pursuit of pleasure and the avoidance of pain. The Roman poet Horace, one of the most-known Latin poets of the Epicurean philosophy, is best known for the words *Carpe diem*. Most people are familiar with Horace's mantra, "Seize the day!" Most people, though, do not know the clause that immediately follows it: *quam minimum credula postero*. This full sentence is translated, "Seize the day, trusting in the future as little as possible." In the Epicurean mindset, a lack of belief in the afterlife led to the pursuit of sensual pleasure as the focus of life.

Whether we call it the YOLO life or Epicureanism, this philosophy pervades modern society. Many college students live with the mentality that "these are the best four years of your life." Believing that all fun and carefree living end once a graduate enters the real world, many young adults plunge into binge drinking, promiscuous behavior, and experimentation with drugs. Adults wrack up massive debt seeking to compile new cars, bigger houses, flashy jewelry, and the latest clothes. People compile bucket lists of vacations and experiences they absolutely must have before they die. The race is on!

For an Epicurean, modern life in the West is an ideal playground. Because of technology and economics, pleasures of all kinds are at any hedonist's fingertips. One can dial up just about anything through the internet. Gourmet foods and fine wines abound. Regular people can take trips to Antarctica, the North Pole, and tropical beaches. The ultra-affluent own private islands. Name your pleasure, and you can have it! Meanwhile, most westerners live in places of relative stability, safety, and affluence in comparison to the conditions of past centuries and the third world.

But here's the problem. Although mankind has never had as much desire for and access to pleasure, many people have never been so miserable. In 2019 the American suicide rate reached an all-time high. The US Centers for Disease Control reported a 33 percent increase in suicides from 1999 to 2019.[1] An American insurance company announced increases in incidents of major depression across every age category from 2013 to 2018.[2] The

---

1 Jamie Ducharme, "U.S. Suicide Rates Are the Highest They've Been Since World War II," *Time*, accessed July 24, 2019, https://time.com/.

2 Maggie Fox, "Major Depression on the Rise among Everyone, New Data Shows," NBC News, accessed July 24, 2019, https://www.nbcnews.com/.

sharpest rise in major depression, which was 63 percent, occurred among American teenagers. People ages fifty to sixty-four had the lowest rate of increase, which was 23 percent.

Aside from empirical data, one only has to look at social media to see the general mood of modern society. People are angry, aggravated, and desperate. Access to pleasure has in no way translated to greater contentment. In fact, it seems to have driven greater dissatisfaction. So many wholeheartedly focus their lives on the excessive pursuit of pleasure only to come up empty-handed. The more we consume, the more empty our souls feel. Certainly an amorphous or nonexistent belief in the afterlife drives so much of this consumption.

As Christians, we are by no means immune from this hedonistic mentality, which Jeremiah Burroughs called "earthly-mindedness."[3] Perhaps this is why so many of our spiritual lives are "meh" and why we lack the joy and enthusiasm that we see emanating from Paul.

What did Paul believe that made his spiritual life so vibrant and exuberant? What did he possess that can bring us greater joy and satisfaction?

Paul's Joyful Contentment in Horrible Circumstances

When one reads Paul's more personal epistles, where he discloses a great deal about his inner life and emotional state, one will find a stark contrast between the dissatisfaction of modern society and the exuberance of Paul. This joyfulness resonates in his letter to the Philippians.

---

3   Jeremiah Burroughs, *Two Treatises of Mr. Jeremiah Burroughs* (Ligonier, PA: Soli Deo Gloria, 1991).

A second layer of this contrast between modern society's mood and Paul's involves his circumstances. While modern westerners have relatively safe, stable, and comfortable lives compared to the rest of mankind throughout history, Paul had awful circumstances. He wrote Philippians from prison with the possibility of impending execution stalking him. Given the joyful tone throughout the letter, one would be shocked to discover that Paul had such miserable circumstances. Paul's heavenly mindedness had much to do with his contentment.

Throughout the letter, Paul uses language of happiness and bliss. He uses the word *joy* five times and the word *rejoice* seven times—hardly the expected vocabulary of a de facto death-row inmate. Paul asked the Philippians to "complete [his] joy by being of the same mind, having the same love, being in full accord and of one mind" (Phil. 2:2), which presupposes that Paul already had a baseline joy of which he seeks completion. Philippians 2:17 captures this paradox of joy amidst suffering, where Paul wrote, "Even if I am to be poured out as a drink offering upon the sacrificial offering of your faith, I am glad and rejoice with you all." Essentially, Paul proclaimed that even the threat of death itself cannot diminish or reduce the bountiful joy in his heart.

Obviously Paul's joy did not originate in pleasant circumstances and material pleasures. He was in prison and expecting death. His contentment flowed from his relationship with Jesus, as he explained in Philippians 3:8–11:

Indeed, I count everything as loss because of the surpassing worth of knowing Christ Jesus my Lord. For his sake I have suffered the loss of all things and count them as rubbish, in order that I may gain Christ and be found in him, not having a righteousness of my own that comes from the law, but that which comes through faith in Christ, the righteousness from God that depends on faith—that I may know him and the power of his resurrection, and may share his sufferings, becoming like him in his death, that by any means possible I may attain the resurrection from the dead.

Paul's great sense of joy flows out of intimacy with Christ. Paul basically says that he will surrender any earthly pleasure, accomplishments, or status in order to have the deeper pleasure and satisfaction of intimacy with Christ. The satisfaction of knowing Christ surpasses the benefits of worldly pleasure to the extent that Paul refers to these earthy goods as "rubbish" or dung. He refers to the joy of knowing Christ as having "surpassing worth," which effectively means that it exceeds human comprehension; it is not of this world.

To use such other-worldly language makes sense because Paul viewed this joy and happiness as being rooted in heaven. Just after expounding upon the vast riches of knowing Christ, Paul makes this declaration:

One thing I do: forgetting what lies behind and straining forward to what lies ahead, I press on toward the goal for the prize of the upward call of God in Christ Jesus. (3:13–14)

Paul does not seek his satisfaction in what is behind or what is below. The trajectory of his heart points toward the "upward call." He sets his heart and mind on heaven above. Paul looks to increase his joy by looking to enjoy the deepest pleasure of heaven: communion with God.

Earlier in Philippians, Paul vacillates between his desire to die and go to heaven and his desire to remain on earth for fruitful service. The apostle describes going to heaven as departing and being with Christ (1:23). Communion with God defines his conceptualization of heaven. One can see the theological foundations of this mindset early in his epistle to the Ephesians. In Ephesians 1:3 Paul wrote, "Blessed be the God and Father of our Lord Jesus Christ, who has blessed us in Christ with every spiritual blessing in the heavenly places." This verse illustrates the nature of Paul's joy-inducing, heavenly spirituality.

First, Paul says that God the Father has blessed believers in Christ. As noted in a previous chapter, when we see this phrase "in Christ," we know that Paul is referring to union with Christ, the oneness and communion with Jesus that results from salvation. One can safely conclude that the usage "in Christ" here means that the instrument through which the Father has delivered spiritual blessings to us is union with Christ.

You may recall that union with Christ can have either past or present implications. In this situation, I believe that both past and present are in play. By being unified with Christ in his life, death, resurrection, and ascension in the past, God has made available to us spiritual blessings now, in the present. Thus, Christ's atoning work washes away our sins and restores communion with God. Simultaneously, we presently access and enjoy these spiritual blessings of heaven via our present union with Christ. The intimate fellowship with the ascended heavenly King constitutes the core of our joy, both in heaven and in this life.

Next, Paul reveals the nature of these blessings. They are spiritual blessings, not material blessings. The foundational, core blessings of our salvation that satisfy our soul are spiritual ones. These blessings involve fellowship with God.

Finally, what is the location or origination of these blessings? The heavenly places. Paul locates the fount of our spiritual blessings in heaven above.

Herein lies one of the great cruelties of the health, wealth, and prosperity heresy. Its proponents point followers down below for their satisfaction. They suggest that Jesus died so that we can multiply our material possessions and worldly comforts. They say "look down" and "look back," while Paul says "look up" and "look ahead" for contentment. These heretics point people away from the true source of contentment and deliver them to deeper emptiness in pursuing satisfaction in empty cisterns.

When you consider the path to a satisfied heart, let the bliss of the saints in heaven guide you in the same way that it did Paul. My little boy, Cam, is perfectly happy in heaven. Keep in mind, in heaven right now he does not live in a material state but in a spiritual, disembodied one. His joy comes from seeing Christ face-to-face, sitting in God's presence, and living in full communion with him. Through union with Christ, God has made this heavenly fellowship available to us, at least in a partial sense. Therefore, we should seek the happiness of heaven by centering our lives on deep intimacy with God.

Looking for Contentment in All the Wrong Places

The secret of Paul's contentment lies not only in his realization of the proper source of joy but also in knowing what will not fulfill him. We as sinners tend to get both wrong. We have seen how Paul views the source of joy as communion with God, patterned after the life of heaven. At the same time, the apostle also had a realistic appraisal of just how happy one can be in this life.

In 2 Corinthians 4 and 5, Paul juxtaposes the struggles of this earthly life with the glories and joys of the life to come in heaven. Here we have dying bodies; there we have glorified ones. Here we have suffering; there we have no pain at all. Here we sin; there we are free and pure in our heart. Paul's catalog of juxtapositions says so much about his realistic expectations for life on this earth.

The gym where I exercise has a sign in the locker room that says, "You can have it all in your lifetime!" Actually, no, you can't. This mantra signifies a core problem with the Epicurean mentality and why so many of us are disenchanted by and discontent in life. We expect to experience the fulfillment of heaven while living in the fallen earth. We expect ultimate happiness while we live with sinful natures and constant self-destruction. We try to find the age to come by digging deeper into the present evil age.

People feel unhappy with where they live, discontent with their job, and dissatisfied with their loved ones. They try to move, find a new career, or get a new significant other. Sometimes, adjusting circumstances is the right move, when God so wills. At the same time, a part of contentment involves having realistic expectations for life. The problem often is not the location, the job, or the other person, but the fact that we live in a dying world.

If you've lost a loved one or experienced a tragedy or even had a stretch of depression, you have tasted the limitations of this fallen world, as well as its pains and sorrows. God uses this suffering to remind us that our hearts are not meant for this world. Heaven will happen fully in heaven, not on the fallen earth, where we live with a bunch of sinners, mainly ourselves.

Management of expectations is a key to happiness. In the fallen world, the happiness of earth will not come close to the happiness our hearts are made for. A practice of contentment involves keeping expectations for life on earth appropriately low.

With this in mind, we must accept with patience the painful realities of life in the fallen world. With the help of the Holy Spirit, we must aim toward Christ—not the material world—for our satisfaction. One cannot attain joy and contentment like Paul's—a heavenly joy—by trying to squeeze juice out of an old, dried-up, desiccated berry.

This mentality leads us to seek Christ here and now more than earthly delights and to live with less FOMO. On a plane ride, I was sitting next to a stranger who told me about all the international trips he and his wife had booked. He admitted that they racked up credit card debt to go on these adventures but justified it by saying, "You only live once." I wanted to say, "No, actually. You'll be able to explore the whole earth free of charge in the new heaven and new earth. You don't need to weary yourself and deplete your finances chasing the restored earth today. Just seek Jesus."

So it is true for us. Sure, we can enjoy the blessings of this life as God leads us. Simultaneously, our greatest contentment comes when we seek deeper fellowship with and vision of Christ every day.

Certainly, God blesses us with happiness and joys through material blessings and experiences. Many of these good blessings in life give us a taste of the new heavens and new earth. Still, these joys apart from fellowship with God cannot touch the bliss of an "upward" kind of intimacy with Jesus. In these realizations, we can find greater joy and contentment with a heaven consciousness.

Your Heavenward Journey

When I think about the life of my little boy in heaven, I have great joy knowing that he is perfectly and perpetually happy. His normal, constant estate of joyful pleasure exceeds the happiest moment I ever shall taste in this life. And yet Cam has absolutely no exposure or access to the material pleasures of this life in heaven today. No food, no sports, no success, no money, no sports cars, no vacations, no candy. He may enjoy some of these physical delights in the new heavens and new earth, but presently in heaven—the intermediate state—we have no biblical suggestion that he experiences material pleasures. Nevertheless, he maintains complete satisfaction and contentment.

How, being separated from all the pleasures of this life, could my son be perfectly happy and permanently exuberant? Quite simply, he fully has God. He lives in undisturbed union with Christ. He sees Jesus face-to-face. He finds complete joy in the presence of the Lord.

As you remember your person in heaven, you can find greater contentment by considering the utter happiness he or she enjoys. Their pleasure comes from fellowship with God and from living in his presence.

The same is true of our Person in heaven, the Lord Jesus. His perfect contentment flows from his communion with the Father and the Holy Spirit.

I am not suggesting that we view the blessings of this life as bad or evil. They are a grace from the Lord. I do think a heavenly mindedness, though, can lead us to greater contentment in this life, as we await the perfect bliss of heaven. Instead of seeking our contentment primarily in the material world and in our circumstances, we can enjoy all the spiritual blessings in the heavenly places that God has given to us through Christ. We can first seek our satisfaction in intimate fellowship with Jesus and by praying to taste his presence. We can pursue the spiritual bliss of heaven first and find the secondary blessings of the material world that much more enriching, as they fall in their proper place.

So let's not settle for and limit ourselves to fleeting pleasures of this life but, instead, seek the future, spiritual pleasures of heaven here in the present.

9

The Transformation
of Heavenward

Sanctification

ANYONE WHO KNOWS ME WELL can tell you that I act like a total nut when I attend Alabama football games. As a passionate, intense fan, I tend to yell too loudly and get too rowdy. A crazy alter ego comes alive when I enter the stadium.

My wife, with much dismay, observed this loud, boisterous persona about a month into marriage. I accidentally knocked over an elderly person when I started jumping up and down after Alabama scored a game-winning touchdown against Arkansas. My new bride understandably was horrified. Perhaps the majority of my most embarrassing behavior has occurred in the stands at football games.

One year, my friend who served as the chief of staff for a congressman called me the night before Alabama's annual battle with

Auburn, the Tide's most intense rival. He said that his boss had come down sick and had given him his two seats in the University of Alabama president's box. Of course, I accepted his invitation.

Let me assure you, my behavior was entirely different for that game. I sat in a new place—not the stands but the skybox of the president of the university. At this game, I was not some anonymous fan in the stands; I was "Michael's friend," which meant that my behavior—for good or ill—reflected upon my buddy. I did not sit in the presence of my usual "good ole boy" acquaintances with whom I ordinarily watched. The president of the entire school sat eight seats over from me. Even the clothes I wore differed. No Alabama apparel and tennis shoes but a blazer, tie, and formal shoes. I did not as much as raise my voice, speak critically, complain about a call, or lose control in any way. The new realm, which included a new location, new identification, and new clothes, radically influenced my more appropriate behavior.

In a similar light, Paul routinely calls for believers to live new, godly lives in response to the radical heavenly shift that has occurred through their conversion. Through faith in Christ, believers now have a new location and, consequently, a new identity and new life. This newness involves a transformation in the moral and ethical dimensions of the believer's life.

Very often Christian teachers present the moral and ethical elements of the Christian life in biblically shallow and incomplete terms. People often hear, "You're a Christian. Here are the rules. Follow them. Do this by trying hard. Oh, maybe get a little help from God along the way." This represents moralism, not biblical sanctification, the latter of which draws on the power of the gospel for inside-out, genuine transformation. Paul's heavenly sanctification portrays a rich, full view of God's way to moral and ethical growth. It draws on the depth of the gospel, including its heavenly dimensions.

The New Life

An interesting trend to observe in Paul's letters involves the frequent connection between heavenly content and moral exhortation. When you see references to heaven and the new heavenly age, moral exhortation often accompanies it. These passages that involve both heavenly content and moral imperatives often contain an emphasis on the new life. This newness involves changes in location and identity. Paul sends a clear message: the new location should naturally result in new everything, including behavior.

We can see this theme vividly in Colossians 3, which begins with one of the richest texts in Scripture about heavenly mindedness and then follows with intense moral exhortation. This passage opens with an encouragement to "seek the things that are above" and to "set [our] minds on things that are above, not on things that are on earth." He justifies this mindset with the reminder that we have been "raised with Christ" (recall that this references union with Christ in his ascension) and that we "have died" (Col. 3:1–3). By having died, he means that we have crossed over one threshold to another. These two phrases emphasize the transfer from the present evil age to the new heavenly age.

Immediately after this call for heavenly mindedness, driven by the eschatological shift, he writes, "Therefore . . . " "Therefore" means that what comes next constitutes a logical response to the prior content. "Put to death therefore what is earthly in you: sexual immorality, impurity, passion, evil desire, and covetousness,

which is idolatry" (3:5). He continues to catalog other sinful behaviors that we should avoid, such as anger, wrath, malice, slander,
obscene talk, and lying (3:8–9). He writes, "In these you too *once
walked*, when you were living in them" (3:7). Paul essentially
communicates that in the old place, the domain of darkness, we
behaved in these immoral ways. But now we are in a new place.
We have gone from general admission to the president's box. We
have gone from the kingdom of darkness into the kingdom of
heaven. The way we live naturally should change based on the
new location.

Paul makes these moral exhortations across all four of the
major heavenly realities that were referenced earlier.[1] In the Colossians 3 passage, he uses language consistent with the new-creation
paradigm. Furthermore, in Ephesians 2:10 when he declares that
"we are [God's] workmanship, created in Christ Jesus for good
works," the creation to which he refers is our new birth into the
new creation. A life of loving service should naturally flow out of
our presence in the new creation.

While the apostle less frequently mentions the light/darkness
paradigm in his letter, he uses it to emphasize the moral implications of the heavenly life. In Ephesians 5:8–9 he writes, "For at
one time you were *darkness*, but now you are *light* in the Lord.
Walk as children of light (for the fruit of light is found in all that
is good and right and true)." In 1 Thessalonians 5:4–5 he encourages believers to live soberly, to be prayerful, and to encourage and
love one another. He reminds them: "You are not in darkness. . . .
We are not of the night." Instead, "you are all children of light,

---

1 Just a reminder: these four paradigms include (1) new creation, (2) kingdom of God,
(3) Spirit/flesh, and (4) light/darkness.

children of the day." This new place, in the light, should mean leaving the old ways behind and walking in godliness.

Paul rarely mentions the "kingdom of God" paradigm without attaching content about morality and ethics. In two cases he lists various sinful behaviors and follows them by saying that those who habitually walk in those ways will not "inherit the kingdom of God" (1 Cor. 6:9–10; Gal. 5:21). In a sense, he suggests that for those who claim to have given their life to Christ, this shift in location should result in a lifestyle change. To continue to walk habitually in sin and to revel in it calls into question whether they actually have moved into the new place through repentance and faith.

Finally, one of the most known examples of Paul associating morality with heavenly places occurs in Galatians 5 where he contrasts walking in the Spirit with walking in the flesh. We often apply this passage about the Spirit and the flesh at the individual level. The flesh refers to our sinful desires; the Spirit refers to living under the power of the Holy Spirit. Remember that Paul thinks about Spirit versus flesh at both the individual and big-picture, eschatological levels. He often refers to the "age of the Spirit," one of the paradigms for the new heavenly age. When Paul instructs believers to "walk by the Spirit," this directive operates at two levels. In one sense, he means that Christians should live in a manner befitting the new heavenly age. The "fruit of the Spirit," which he lists in this passage, describes the attributes that emanate through a person living in God's heavenly place (5:22–23). These attributes demonstrate how we will perpetually glorify God in heaven. At the same time, to walk by the Spirit also means to rely on the power of the Holy Spirit, which, of course, is a major blessing for believers in the new heavenly age. He wrote, "If we live by the Spirit, let us also keep in step with the Spirit" (5:25). To live in the age of the Spirit means to no longer rely on our own inner strength but instead to live with a heavenly awareness and with a dependence on the Holy Spirit.

These connections mean that we can consider Christian morality with a top-down mentality. We can ask, "Am I going to act or think like this when I get to heaven?" Knowing what we know about our transfer into the new heavenly age through our conversion, we logically can deduce that we already have reached glory in one sense. Thus, a heavenly lifestyle in our present life makes sense. The ways of heaven should be the ways of today.

Obviously, we still remain connected to the old age through our sinful flesh and presence in the fallen world, so I do not mean to say that we will cease to struggle with sin. Until God delivers us from this earth, we will constantly struggle with sin. We will have to rely on the Holy Spirit to walk in God's ways. We daily will have to repent frequently and seek Christ's forgiveness and restoration.

Simultaneously, Paul demonstrates a mindset toward sanctification that is far richer than what most believers naturally possess. The apostle presents what I would call "eschatological sanctification," which draws on the fullness of the gospel, including all of the heavenly realities, to bless us with all the resources of our salvation for our struggle with sin and pursuit of godliness.

These connections between the new heavenly location and Christian character do not simply work at the intellectual level. Paul does not simply say, "Remember that you live in heaven. Now be good." I can tell you from my own spiritual life that simply recalling spiritual truths apart from relationship with God and his grace carries limited power in our battle to resist sin and to live loving, godly lives. The apostle reminds us of all the power, grace, and blessings that come with our transfer to the new heavenly age and how they aid us in faithfully following Christ.

The new place reminds us of the new identity we have gained in Christ. As part of the aforementioned Colossians 3 exhortation, Paul proclaims, "Do not lie to one another, seeing that you have put off the *old self* with its practices and have put on the *new self*, which is being renewed in knowledge after the image of its creator" (3:9–10). We have a new self. We are now righteous and forgiven through the blood of Christ. We are now adopted children of God and coheirs with Christ (Rom. 8:17). Personal experience tells us that when we have security in our identity, we tend to be less self-consumed and more loving. We tend to be less apt to brag or prove ourselves or talk trash when we have a solid sense of self-worth grounded in God's love.

Also, not only do we have the Holy Spirit as a benefit of our new heavenly place; we also have the transforming power of union with Christ. Paul draws frequent connections between union with Christ and sanctification. He alludes to the Corinthians as those "sanctified *in Christ*" (1 Cor. 1:2).[2] He directs Timothy to be "strengthened by the grace that is *in Christ Jesus*" (2 Tim. 2:1). He encourages the Ephesians to be "strong *in the Lord*" as they resist the spiritual forces of evil (Eph. 6:10). Union with Christ constitutes a central blessing of the heavenly experience. Enjoying joyful, intimate fellowship with Jesus, as we will perpetually

2 Recall that phrases such as "in Christ," "in the Lord," and "in Christ Jesus" refer to union with Christ.

in heaven, strengthens us and puts our lives under the control of God. The heavenly benefit of present union with Christ plays a major role in our sanctification.

Finally, the eternal perspective of setting our minds on things above and not on earthly things sanctifies us. Short-sighted, earthly mindedness drives so much greed and corruption. When I see preachers who pander false gospels to needy people while owning private jets, fancy cars, and multiple mansions, I wonder, "Do you have any awareness that you're going to face God for your life? Is the short-term pleasure of your greed and material-ism really worth selling your birthright?" The same can be said of people who compromise ethics and relationships at all costs in the name of excessive, material gain. When people remember that they will inherit the earth with Christ at the second coming, they do not focus on satisfying their greedy, corrupt appetite for immediate gratification. They can defer those pleasures until the new heaven and earth and avoid these damaging patterns of sin.

In sum, heavenly truths remind us of the goodness of God and the fullness of the gospel. When you meditate on and savor these present and future heavenly blessings, it will draw you closer to the Lord. It will lead you to trust in Jesus and his grace, the very faith which transforms our lives.

Pleasure and Self-Control

A critical element of the role of heaven in our sanctification re-volves around our conception of pleasure. When we hear the word *pleasure*, we often have negative associations. We can think that pleasure equals sin. In reality, pleasure is from God. However, our sinful nature leads us to pursue it through idols. Seeing heaven as the source of all true, godly pleasure helps aid our struggle against sin and leads us to abundant life in Christ.

Paul often characterizes the lifestyle of the old age with descriptions of sensual pleasure. In Romans 13 when he discusses the sin of the "darkness" and the "night," he mentions orgies, drunkenness, sexual immorality, fits of anger, and sensuality (Rom. 13:12–13). All of these sins involve misdirected, sinful pleasure. They characterize a hedonistic lifestyle. As we discussed in the introduction and chapter 8, hedonism naturally flows out of a worldview with no real, clear afterlife. Paul writes in 1 Corinthians 15:32, "If the dead are not raised, 'Let us eat and drink, for tomorrow we die.'" In other words, if there is no resurrection of the dead and no hopeful afterlife, then the pragmatic response is to live a life of sensual pleasure.

Accounts of the last days of Hitler's bunker and the Third Reich Chancellery depict a raucous scene of sex and drunkenness. Certain doom was pending. The people presumedly had no joyful hope of a heavenly afterlife. So what made sense as the dreaded Red Army closed in on Berlin? Immerse oneself in uninhibited pleasure to numb the reality that nothing eternally good resides on the other side.

In this conversation about heaven and pleasure, Paul would likely lead us to look to what God has revealed in Scripture about the joys of heaven as the guide to true, sustainable, life-giving pleasure. Again, what will make heaven *heaven*? Primarily, seeing Christ and enjoying perfect fellowship with God.

You know what will absolutely not be a part of the pleasure of heaven? Sin. We will not sin in heaven. Sin impedes our fellowship with God and obscures our vision of Christ. Sin leads us away from the deepest pleasure our heart can possess. Paul would probably reason with us: "You live in the new heavenly place, and you now have access to the pleasures of heaven in fellowship with Christ. Sin makes no sense." Instead, we would be advised to pursue the pleasures of intimacy with God and seeing Jesus, which are more satisfying, while repenting from sin.

This conversation about heaven has critical relevance in both secular and Christian worlds today. We live in a society obsessed with pleasure of various forms. One need look no further than modern reality-television, where the lives of characters frequently revolve around nothing more than sexual hookups, getting drunk, wild parties, and luxurious possessions. The insane arguments, trolling, and rants of social media, such as Twitter and internet forums, reflect this pervasive hedonism. There's a backward visceral pleasure in yelling and screaming and arguing and condemning on the internet.

In today's world this unfiltered celebration of worldly pleasure is particularly strong in the realm of sexuality. Media and advertisers have sexualized just about every facet of life. They even sexualize hamburger commercials and mascara brands! Youth-based sex education shies away from abstinence as a viable possibility. Pop psychology supports sexual activity of just about any kind as healthy and authentic. However, Scripture calls for believers to live lives of self-restraint.

Here's the hard news: in the realm of sexuality, unless God calls a man and a woman into marriage, they are called to maintain celibacy. Yes, as crazy as it may sound in the modern world, God calls some people not to be sexually active for the entirety of their lives. (Let's not forget that Jesus was never sexually active, and he lived the most fruitful, flourishing life ever.)

With that being said, calling for such abstinence for unmarried people—and for young people—without offering them the hope of both present and future heaven is not only biblically incomplete; it is cruel. If people do not have the expectation of the consummation of pleasure for eternity in heaven, they will feel as if they are completely missing out on the best that human existence has to offer. In reality, there will be no sex in heaven (Matt. 22:30). The pleasures of the vision of Christ and perfect fellowship with God far exceed any pleasure on earth, including sexual pleasure. No matter the worldly pleasure we may long for in this life, when we get to heaven none of us will feel that we missed out because we did not smoke weed or sleep around or spend money extravagantly. In fact, we will look at those activities as cheap, empty, and foolish compared to the ultimate pleasure of enjoying Jesus. There will be no FOMO in heaven!

The best way to abstain from sinful sensuality is to pursue the satisfaction of our desires in fellowship with Christ; in other words, seeking pleasure that actually satisfies. Heavenly mindedness guides us in this pursuit. When Paul twice references the "eternal life in Christ" that has come to us through the gospel, he is talking about the satisfying quality of heavenly life now in relationship with Jesus. He is talking about enjoying heavenly pleasure in the present in a manner that actually edifies us (Rom. 6:22–23). Stephen Nichols described Jonathan Edwards's Christian spirituality along these lines. He wrote, "Edwards's pleasure argument tells us something about living in between. It tells us that as citizens of heaven, we are to bring heaven, with all of its joy and delights, pleasure and sweetness, to earth."[3] Indeed, seeking heavenly pleasure in the present mitigates our appetite for sinful sensuality.

Though the struggle to resist sinful temptations involves much pain and failure (for which God offers abundant mercy), pursuing heavenly pleasures in Christ, here and now, strengthens us in this aim. Heavenly blessings point us to life-giving, God-centered pleasure that edifies us rather than harms us, like sinful sensuality does.

Your Heavenward Journey

In all of this talk of sanctification and moral exhortation, there is a heavenly word of comfort we very much need. We all have those areas of sin that plague us, that we just cannot seem to shake—areas where we long for "progress" and deliverance but there seems to be a daily return to square one. Constant failure after repentance stands as one of the more painful experiences of life in human flesh.

I've struggled with a bad (and at times explosive) temper as long as I can remember. I knew from age seven, when I started playing sports, that I had a problem with anger. I would have spectacular tantrums when I failed or lost. These issues with anger were manifested when I started driving, and I would "scream" at what I deemed to be bad drivers. When my wife and I started having children, I found myself with a short fuse when my sweet children disrespected or defied me. Every time I lapse into anger, I feel incredible regret and disappointment.

Thirty-four years after that initial conviction of sin, I cannot say that I've observed much progress. I have had low-grade road

3 Stephen J. Nichols, *Heaven On Earth: Capturing Jonathan Edwards's Vision of Living in Between* (Wheaton, IL: Crossway, 2006), 50.

rage with my kids in the car. When my favorite sports team loses or gets a bad call or when I hit a really bad golf shot, I'm just as prone to losing my temper and yelling as when I was a teenager. Perhaps the only progress I have experienced is deeper awareness and conviction over my sin in this one area. There has been no lack of effort, no shortage of prayers, no deficiency of desire, and no absence of conviction. For whatever reason, I just haven't changed very much.

Paul knew this struggle himself. In 2 Corinthians 12 he wrote about the thorn in his flesh, a compulsive and persistent bondage to sin that he could not shake. (A great deal of speculation has surrounded this text, as people have tried to guess the nature of his ailment. Some believe, including me, that Paul speaks of a spiritual struggle with sin, but we don't really know much from the text.)

We all have at least one and usually several areas of sin struggle where we feel discouraged and are not seeing any life change. For so many people, addiction represents this challenge in their lives. They've gone to more AA meetings than they could ever count, and they've never received that one-year chip. They've been in and out of rehab ten times, swearing on each occasion, "This time it's gonna be different," only to relapse yet again. They've read dozens of books about pornography addiction, checked in with a sponsor daily, and set up an armed fortress of restrictions on technology, yet that burning desire to look at porn has never been overcome.

Paul has good news for struggling sinners: God's grace is sufficient for you and me (2 Cor. 12:9). Period. The persistence of our sins can never outpace or delete the mercy of Jesus reckoned to us by God through Christ. There will be a day in this journey when we no longer sin. When we experience our glorification upon entry into heaven, God will purify our nature such that we never sin ever again. Never. Not one more time. No more regrets. No more emotional hangovers.

These struggles also extend to relationships with others, where we desire to live in love and harmony but tension seems to dominate. My father experienced much tension with his mother throughout his relationship with her. He told me about some of the struggles he experienced in that relationship. Surely we all want peaceful, loving relationships with our family, but often those are the bonds that cause some people the most pain. On his deathbed as we talked about heaven, I told my father, "Soon you're going to see your mother, and you'll both be without sin. You're going to love and accept each other in a way that you never did."

We can look forward to the day when we relate to our loved ones with no sin at all. No judgment, no anger, no using, no fear, no unkindness, no sarcasm. All of those sorrowful regrets I carry about not perfectly loving my son, Cam, taking him for granted, or being harsh out of frustration—they will all be gone. And I will love and enjoy him in a way I never could due to my sinful flesh.

These days of struggle are limited. The day of glory will come. The misery of sinning will be over. And you can take an eternal sigh of relief because heaven means that the struggle is no more.

10

The Strength of Heavenward

Hope

ONE WILL SCARCELY FIND a more horrific, excruciating life experience in history than that of slaves in the United States. They were abducted by force from Africa, shipped on boats in filthy, inhumane conditions, and then sold like cattle. Once they became slaves, their daily rhythm became that of endless toil, abuse, and dehumanization. Slave owners could sell them and separate them from their families at a moment's notice. They lived in shacks and were fed the leftover scraps. They were locked into this horror for life. There was essentially no possibility of release or freedom. In circumstantial terms, the slave had no hope in life.

How does one cope, how does one basically survive, when life is guaranteed misery with no expectation of relief?

Theologian Howard Thurman described the life of slaves as so "cheap" that their death was merely "a matter of bookkeeping" in the eyes of their owners.[1] He wrote that a primary means through which slaves survived was the singing of spirituals. In his published work *The Negro Spiritual Speaks of Life and Death*, Thurman identified the theme of heaven as central in the songs of slaves. He asserted the constant singing of heaven provided the foundational means of their perseverance and survival. Thurman wrote, "With such an affirmation ringing in the ears, it became possible for them, slaves though they were, to stand anything that life could bring against them."[2]

The promise of heaven provided these human beings, for whom suffering defined existence, to endure and prevail during a journey of perpetual pain. The refrain of the songs became the refrain of heaven in their minds and in their lives.

In the spiritual "I'm A-Travelin' to the Grave," the stanzas recount the deaths of the speaker's wife, brother, and sister. As they die, each person shouts and screams, "Glory hallelujah!" Their last words were "about Jerusalem," or the new Jerusalem, the city of God in heaven. There is a sense of celebration and victory in their death. There is the expression of "Finally, at last!"

The chorus of this song demonstrates how these people framed life in terms of eternity. The chorus repeats:

I'm a-trav'ling to the grave,
I'm a-trav'ling to the grave, my Lord,
I'm a-trav'ling to the grave,
For to lay this body down.

1 Howard Thurman, *The Negro Spiritual Speaks of Life and Death* (Richmond, IN: Friends United Press, 1975), 13–14.
2 Thurman, *The Negro Spiritual*, 24.

Each difficult day was situated within a journey to heaven.

In another song, "Wait a Little While," the speaker shows how heaven provides a perspective that makes the horrors of life appear possible to endure. He sings:

Wait a little while,
Then we'll sing a new song,
Wait a little while,
Then we'll sing a new song

Sometimes I get a heavenly view,
then we'll sing a new song
And then my trials are few,
Then we'll sing a new song.

The promise of singing a "new song" in heaven enables him to tell his suffering neighbor, "Just wait a little while longer; we are going to make it home to see Jesus. We are going to prevail." When he considers heaven, his trials, which are immense, start to appear "few."

American slaves did not have to exert discipline in order to have an eternal mindset. Heaven was not merely a nice thing to consider from time to time. Heavenly mindedness served as the basis of basic, existential survival.

These themes in American slave spirituals resemble Paul's mentality of drawing hope from heaven in order to endure the trials and travails of life. After his conversion, Paul's life became one of virtually continual pain.[3] Suffering followed the apostle. Paul was

---

3 This transition is not meant to suggest that I am comparing Paul's sufferings to that of American slaves. I am not sure that such a comparison is really fair or possible on either side.

blinded for three days. He lived during famine. He was unjustly arrested multiple times. He was hated to the point that people wanted to murder him. He was beaten and flogged naked in public. He lived under house arrest for several years. He endured a shipwreck. He was left for dead at one point. He knew poverty. He endured immense trauma. He was misunderstood, resisted, and betrayed. He saw people that he invested in fall away from the faith. In the end, the government executed him, perhaps by beheading.

Paul knew the full spectrum of human suffering to the most intense degree. Nevertheless, in all of this, he demonstrated an inexplicable buoyancy through his life. God buoyed his soul through the hope of heaven.

The writing of Paul's second letter to Corinth came during a time of particularly intense difficulty. While Paul suffered, he expressed a sense of resiliency as well. He wrote:

> We are afflicted in every way, but not crushed; perplexed, but not driven to despair; persecuted, but not forsaken; struck down, but not destroyed; always carrying in the body the death of Jesus, so that the life of Jesus may also be manifested in our bodies. (2 Cor. 4:8–10)

He faced the whole constellation of human misery, and yet Paul was not "crushed," hopeless, "destroyed," nor alone. He did not soft-peddle or minimize the pain he experienced. Simultaneously, he continued to move forward with strength and hope.

One can attribute so much of this resilience to the hope of heaven that he references in this same passage. Paul viewed these trials in the context of moving toward heaven. He wrote that our "outer self is wasting away"; our bodies decay as they move toward death. Meanwhile, "our inner self is being renewed day by day" (2 Cor. 4:16). God is sanctifying our heart as we move closer and closer to our full glorification in heaven. Paul took heart in the reality, in 2 Corinthians 5:1, that "if the tent that is our earthly home is destroyed, we have a building from God, a house not made with hands, eternal in the heavens." The earthly tent refers to his earthly body, while the "building from God" alludes to his place in heaven, more specifically his resurrected body in the new heaven and new earth. The worst thing that can befall Paul is to die and end up with God in heaven.

In particular, heaven provided two critical principles that sustained him. First, heaven provided a perspective on time that enabled endurance. Paul referred to the extreme and perpetual trials that he faced as light and momentary afflictions (2 Cor. 4:17). Light and momentary? Can you recall the worst year of your life? I remember the year after my child died. Each day felt like a week and each week like a month. Paul, though, had such a profound eternal mindset that his continual afflictions felt brief.

Eternity made the time of his struggles seem short, but the relative greatness of his anticipated joy in heaven made the pains feel light or, better said, lighter. Paul said that the suffering of this life is "preparing for us an eternal weight of glory" (4:17). In other words, he felt like the happiness and euphoria and fulfillment of heaven reached such ultimate heights that the depths of pain in this life seemed relatively manageable. Consequently, the apostle declared firmly, "We do not lose heart" (4:16).

Meditating on the glories of heaven served as Paul's greatest asset in enduring suffering, and it stands as our greatest asset too. Puritan John Owen wrote, "Nothing is more useful [in enduring trials] than contemplations of eternal things and future glory."[4] Indeed, I have found this statement to be true.

The more I thought about eternity after Cam's death, the more manageable the trial felt. There were moments when I wondered if the rest of my days would be filled with grief and sadness. I didn't know if healing could emerge from such sorrow. Even when I had those dreadful thoughts, eternity made the prospect of enduring chronic grief seem plausible. The intensity of heaven made the magnitude of my sorrow feel "a little less bad," such that surviving seemed conceivable.

God has given me much healing and relief from my tragedy such that I generally have a happy, contented life these days. However, many people live in virtually constant pain. Some people live with chronic back pain or with a never-ending headache. Others suffer from intense mental health conditions from which they never get a break; the depression or psychosis or anxiety never stops. For others a constant battle with addiction plagues them. When they wake up, the physical cravings and mental obsessions visit them. A battle exists daily.

Because Christ has opened the door of heaven, the battle will end. The pain will cease. If you live with chronic pain, know that you will not always be bonded to this agony.

This hope can provide the strength you need to endure the next moment, one step at a time. As great as heaven will be, this

---

4 John Owen, *Sin and Grace*, vol. 7, *The Works of John Owen* (London: Banner of Truth, 1965), 323.

life is worth living and this struggle worth enduring. Given how much I have played up heaven, I think I must make this statement: If taking your life has ever entered your mind, please take heart, God can carry you through the darkness. Infinite years of pain-free happiness await you in eternity. As grueling and as long as your struggle surely feels, the hope of heaven can supply the grace you need to endure today and tomorrow. Again, if you are thinking about self-harm, you should immediately contact a pastor, friend, or mental health professional.

The chorus of American slave spirituals provides a hopeful refrain for life. These songs employ a repetition of eternity. The stanzas may travel into the challenges of life and the laments of suffering, but the chorus brings the hope of eternity back to mind, back to the forefront of life.

Even the person with the most comfortable life in this world still suffers to an almost unbearable degree. The disproportionately high suicide rates among wealthy Americans validate this reality. I once said to an older priest, "I think most people in the pews on a normal bad day live a step and a half away from suicide." He said, "I think it's more like a half step."

Not to be overly cynical or dramatic, but life is hard. It's really, really hard for every person in the fallen earth. Singing the chorus of heaven in our hearts and our minds is essential for persevering with hope. This very practice can help you not only to endure but to flourish in your suffering.

The Hope of God's Judgment

So far in talking about the hope that heaven provides in suffering, we have emphasized the relief of being delivered from this world and the eternal bliss that will infinitely exceed the trials of this life. An element of the second coming of Christ provides great hope to some people in an unexpected way.

When we think about the hope of heaven, we tend to think about the happiness of seeing Christ and the experience of perfect union with God. The outpouring of God's wrath at the final judgment does not typically first come to mind—unless you are a person living under excruciating injustice and oppression.

In 2 Thessalonians Paul addressed a group of people under intense, persistent persecution for their faith. Given the heightened suffering they encountered, Paul worried that they might lose their faith. In an attempt to give them hope, the initial terms Paul used to comfort them included "repay with affliction," "inflicting vengeance," "flaming fire," and "punishment of eternal destruction" (2 Thess. 1:6, 8–9). Wow! That's hopeful! If you were a persecuted member of the church at Thessalonica, yes, this element of the end times absolutely imbued hope and perseverance.

Language of divine vengeance and eternal judgment can make majority-culture people like me uncomfortable. I have typically lived in situations where my faith is accepted or affirmed. I have never really been a victim of injustice or oppression; the systems have always worked for me. However, if you are an oppressed victim of injustice, like the Thessalonians, then the promise of God's judgment gives you the assurance you need to carry on.

In 1963 some Ku Klux Klansmen planted a bomb loaded with dynamite in the children's wing of the 16th Street Baptist Church in Birmingham, Alabama. It was "youth Sunday" at that church. The blast killed four little girls. If that was your daughter, your granddaughter, your sister, your cousin, or your best friend, how could you trust in the goodness of God and remain faithful, knowing that you will never see justice in this life? Due to the atrocious injustices of the Jim Crow South, if you were a black person in Birmingham in 1963, you knew that there was no way that the government would ever bring the perpetrators who murdered those innocent children to justice.

Throughout history many Christians have lived in situations where they've experienced oppression, imprisonment, torture, and even murder for their faith. Today, in nations like North Korea and Afghanistan, believers who encounter such oppression know they will never see justice because the government, the people charged to uphold justice, is the very body oppressing them.

For victims of oppression without any hope of justice in this life, the promise of God's judgment is critical to their faith. For people with this life experience, the challenge they face in trusting God involves wondering how the Lord can be good in the midst of such atrocities with impunity. They wonder how God can truly love them when they see no sign of justice.

In passages of Scripture where God expresses the fullness of his wrath, in books such as Obadiah, Nahum, 2 Thessalonians, and Revelation, God reminds victims of oppression that his justice will prevail in the end. The very end. On the day of the Lord.

The promise of God's final judgment helps all people who suffer in the fallen world. When we look at the news and see dictators who massacre innocent people for power, drug lords who ruin thousands of people's lives in order to get rich, and perpetrators who prey on the vulnerability of women and children, we cry, "Where are you, God? How can you let this happen?" We despair in the pain of this world and question the goodness of God.

In promising divine vengeance and final judgment, God communicates to those who suffer and lament, "I see you. I see your pain. I see the wrongs of this life, and I will make them all right at the end of time when I return. In the meantime, you can trust me."

Certainly both the Lord and we ourselves desire that perpetrators of injustice would repent and receive the forgiveness of God. Simultaneously, for the uncorrected wrongs of this world, a heavenly hope abides that the Lord will rectify all injustice at the second coming.

The Love of Heaven Heals All Pains

Perhaps some saints in glory guess the truth,
    Perhaps some angels read it as they move,
And cry one to another full of ruth,
    "Her heart is breaking for a little love."
    Though other things have birth,
    And leap and sing for mirth,
When spring-time wakes and clothes and feeds the earth.

Yet saith a saint: "Take patience for thy scathe";
    Yet saith an angel: "Wait, for thou shalt prove
True best is last, true life is born of death,
    O thou, heart-broken for a little love!
    Then love shall fill thy girth,
    And love make fat thy dearth,
When new spring builds new heaven and clean new earth."

In this incredibly personal poem about a woman suffering in isolation, Christina Rossetti laments the pains of outwardly looking fine but inwardly suffering deep depression and loneliness. The refrain in the first four stanzas is essentially, "My heart is breaking for a little love." Though the scenes of spring surround her and the lifelessness of winter has passed, in her interior life, the speaker longs for just "a little love."

In stanzas 5 and 6, which are cited above, the speaker's heart turns to heaven. In stanza 5 she wonders if those above understand her anguish, unlike those around her. She questions, "Perhaps some saints in glory guess the truth, / Perhaps some angels read it as they move, / And cry one to another full of ruth, / "Her heart is breaking for a little love." The hope of possibly being seen, known, and understood provides some comfort while she languishes in the cruel misery of alienation and feeling unloved.

Great hope comes in the end when she finds ultimate comfort. The saints and angels exhort her to "take patience" and to "wait" with certain expectation that "heart-broken for a little love" will be filled. When? When the ultimate, eternal spring of "new heaven and clean new earth" come. At that point, "Then love shall fill thy girth, / And love make fat thy dearth," meaning that her heart's need for love will be perfectly satisfied and her lacking turned to bounty.

At the bottom of our pains in this life is the greatest ailment, that one lost when Eden mankind besmirched. There in Eden, Adam and Eve knew perfect love. Sin had not stained human relationship, so they knew and loved and understood and cared for each other without sin. They were in perfect harmony with God and lived under and experienced his perfect affection. They knew no loneliness or disconnect. They felt no depression.

We cannot imagine such a state. We all live with insecurities, fears, and wounds. We all harbor varying elements of self-loathing and bear secret sins, abuses, and shames. We all wonder, "If I never picked up the phone, would anyone ever call me? If I couldn't do x, y, and z, would anybody truly like me, much less love me?"

Every heart this side of glory, when the moments still, no duties stand before us, no sounds of others are around, and devices shut down, resounds the refrain, "My heart is breaking for a little love." No love in this world will suffice or satisfy the deepest longing of our hearts. Our hearts were made for perfect love and perfect fellowship. Nothing short of this standard will quench the pain and yearning, and nothing close to this standard will come to us in the fallen earth.

Yes, we have moments when we feel the perfect love of God in our lives. Perhaps in prayer, communion, worship, or Scripture we drink small cups from this fountain of God's complete, pure affection, but those sweet yet tenuous moments pass thinly. We have moments when Jesus visits us in the kindness of others and we experience his heavenly grace. But those moments are occasional and fleeting. A measure of mercy, appetizers of the full, constant, perfect love of God in heaven.

There in his heavenly presence his perfect, complete love fills our hearts and quenches the inner agony that all residents of the present evil age endure, however aware or unaware they may be. In the unfettered, unveiled presence of the Father all inner agonies dissipate and disappear. The self-doubt is answered. The voices of shame silenced. The sense of deep inadequacy washed clean. The abuses and violations healed. The loneliness vanished. Addictions cured. Sins forgiven.

These realities of perfect love and knowledge do dwell with us now in Christ, but we only taste them in small, partial, unique sips in the fallen world while in flesh. Paul expressed this notion and tension well in 1 Corinthians 13:12: "For now we see in a mirror dimly, but then face to face. Now I know in part; then I shall know fully, even as I have been fully known."

Then, as Rossetti wrote, in the full heavenly presence of Christ, "love shall fill thy girth, / And love make fat thy dearth." Being loved and understood and accepted and adored and cherished shall be a sustained norm, our waking and sleeping for all times when we dwell with the Father in heaven. The moment in this life where we felt most loved will be exceeded and magnified and sustained.

Forever.

Your Heavenward Journey

The scenes of suffering in our lives can overwhelm us. So often the scenery of life feels like nothing but images of pain. We struggle to see the light at the end of the tunnel. We question, "God, where is the good in any of this?" In these moments, finding a way forward seems impossible.

In these dark times, I often ask myself, "How would Cam view this difficult circumstance, given what he can see in heaven?" Cam can see God in his full glory. He witnesses the full goodness, purity, and wisdom of the Almighty God. He has the perspective of eternity.

I do not think that my son looks down upon my life. While some find it sentimentally comforting, in reality, our loved ones above are not watching our day-to-day lives. God has delivered them from the fallen world, and they spend their days worshiping and gazing upon Jesus.

However, if I could talk to Cam in these moments, I believe he would say, "Oh, Dad, if you could see the beauty of the Lord

God as I do now, you would know what I know: it's all going to be okay. You're going to make it." As I think about the heavenly vision of God, my problems, which seem overwhelming, begin to shrink, even if just a small bit.

The sight of God will assuage all concern and provide ultimate comfort. Until that day, ask the Lord to bless you with a vision of his precious Son with all of his radiance. Imagine the sight of Christ in heaven. Know that viewing your circumstances with a vision of the heavenly Jesus in the background makes them seem so much smaller and so much more manageable.

A day will come when God frees us from the sufferings of this life. That hope can supply much strength to help you endure.

In that day of deliverance, you will no longer have to walk by faith but instead will walk by sight. Walking by sight means you will see the full goodness of Jesus in all his majestic glory.

When you see the glorious Christ, all these sufferings will make sense.

When you see the glorious Christ, you will know the ultimate truth: all is well, and all will be well.

11

The Motivation of Heavenward

Service

A MYTHICAL ACCUSATION often lobbed at heavenly mindedness is summed up in this Oliver Wendell Holmes quote: "Some people are so heavenly minded that they are of no earthly good." Based on both my experience and the witness of Scripture and church history, I would candidly apprise Holmes's position as mostly nonsense.

C. S. Lewis once basically said the opposite in *Mere Christianity*. He wrote:

> If you read history you will find that the Christians who did most for the present world were just those who thought most of the next. . . . It is since Christians have largely ceased to think of the other world that they have become so ineffective in this. Aim at Heaven and you will get earth "thrown in": aim at earth and you will get neither.[1]

---

1   C. S. Lewis, *Mere Christianity* (London: William Collins, 2012), 134.

I side with C. S. Lewis 100 percent. After Cam died and my heavenward journey began, my new heavenly mindedness impacted my view of missions and evangelism as much as any other area of life. As relayed in the book *Therefore I Have Hope*,[2] I struggled a great deal with the meaning of life in the months after Cam passed away. I did not want to be on this earth; I wanted to be with God and my son. While I was not suicidal, I questioned the point of life and would have been content for a Mack Truck to run me over.

One night I had a mystical experience, where I felt as if the Lord had called my bluff. During that entire day I repeatedly lamented that I saw no point in staying alive. In this moment on my bed, I felt as if the Lord said to me, "I can take you right now, if I choose to." It felt so real, as if the door of death stood at my bedside, and if I slid off the mattress I would pass through it. Right then, all I could think about was serving my family and sharing the gospel with people who have not received it. When I questioned the meaning of my existence, and when the afterlife felt imminent, my mind immediately turned to evangelism and service. Since that time, as heavenly mindedness has increased in my life, so has my focus and motivation for serving God and advancing his kingdom. In the moments when eternity feels most real, my concern for God's mission and glory feels most high.

Paul's mind turned in a similar direction in Philippians, when he lived in the terrifying mystery of whether he would live or die. He admitted that he wanted to go to be with the Lord; that would be the fulfillment of his deepest desires. However, he defined

---

2   Cameron Cole, *Therefore I Have Hope: 12 Truths That Comfort, Sustain, and Redeem in Tragedy* (Wheaton, IL: Crossway, 2018).

staying on this earth as "more necessary" for the sake of "fruitful labor" (Phil. 1:22–24). The thing that tied him to life on earth was serving the Lord and advancing the gospel.

Certain factors in his heavenward mindset created this missional focus. These same factors absolutely can heighten your passion and conviction for God's kingdom and glory too, since they are all true of your salvation as well.

Heavenward Factors That Create Missional Focus

In his letters, Paul makes several very similar statements demonstrating his acute anticipation of the second coming of Christ. It's as if Paul lived with a continual consciousness that *this could be the day!*

He once prayed for the church in Philippi, "It is my prayer that your love may abound more and more, with knowledge and all discernment, so that you may approve what is excellent, and so be pure and blameless for the day of Christ" (Phil. 1:9–10). He similarly prayed for the church at Thessalonica, "May the Lord make you increase and abound in love for one another and for all . . . so that he may establish your hearts blameless in holiness before our God and Father, at the coming of our Lord Jesus with all his saints" (1 Thess. 3:12–13). This awareness of the second coming moved him to think about his lifestyle, particularly a life of sacrificial love and service.

As much as any other response, his mind turned to missions and service. In the passages where the apostle's focus turned to kingdom work, we can identify several themes.

First, Paul's heavenward, missional attitude exhibited a great sense of urgency. In 1 Corinthians he recommended that single people remain single if at all possible, because "the unmarried man is anxious about the things of the Lord, how to please the Lord" (1 Cor. 7:32). In contrast, the married person has to worry about his or her family. Paul exalted singleness because it facilitated maximal focus on gospel ministry. His justification for this sentiment involved our limited time on earth: "This is what I mean, brothers: the appointed time has grown very short. From now on, let those who have wives live as though they had none. . . . For the present form of this world is passing away" (7:29–31).

One thing to consider, brothers and sisters, is that there are only two things that you can do on earth that you cannot do in heaven: sin and evangelize. The only good thing that we lose in our transition to glory is the opportunity to share the gospel with the lost. This startling reminder should naturally jolt and awaken us to an urgent sense of prayer and intentionality for those who do not know the glorious saving grace of God. We want to fight off complacency and not presume that tomorrow will always come.

Second, Paul's eternal ministry mindset recognized that a quality exists in the way we live our lives with respect to serving God. In 1 Corinthians 3:12–15 he wrote:

> Now if anyone builds on the foundation with gold, silver, precious stones, wood, hay, straw— each one's work will become manifest, for the Day will disclose it, because it will be revealed by fire, and the fire will test what sort of work each one has done. If the work that anyone has built on the foundation survives, he will receive a reward. If anyone's work is burned up, he will suffer loss, though he himself will be saved, but only as through fire.

To be clear, this passage does not refer to salvation. Eternal salvation does not depend on works; it relies entirely on grace alone through faith alone. Simultaneously, we can see that Paul had an awareness that some can invest their lives in kingdom ministry better than others. The gradient of gold and silver to hay and straw highlights this discrepancy in quality. Furthermore, the quality of that investment would become evident at the second coming of Christ.

What may this look like? In one case, a person may have received Christ as Lord and Savior and yet live a self-consumed life that largely focuses on personal comfort, material gain, frequent entertainment, and being served by others. Such a person may be saved but does not steward his time, talent, or treasure much for the advancement of the kingdom. On the contrary, out of the power and grace of the Holy Spirit, another person may focus her life on serving others, sharing the gospel, giving generously, seeking justice, relieving the poor, and praying for people and the world. The latter life contains greater quality from an eternal perspective. That life submits to God's work of advancing the kingdom. Paul says that quality will result in reward at the second coming. The apostle would say, too, that the deeds themselves do not, in and of themselves, gain reward; it's the heart that desires to love, honor, and glorify God that does. The motivation contributes to the quality.

We can all identify with days in our lives that possess greater kingdom value than others. We know our hearts. We know when we've lived a day consumed with our own comforts, aggrandizement, and entitlements. We also know the feeling of a day lived close to the Lord, when we have a great desire to please him and when God works through us. Given the depth of our sin, we struggle to know the purity of our motivations. At the same time, we can admit our sinful and selfish tendencies to God and ask the Spirit to help us operate out of purer motivation.

The third motivating factor, which we touched on briefly above, involved the expectation of rewards. Geerhardus Vos commented, regarding Paul's focus on reward in heaven, "On the basis of the available evidence alone there can be no doubt as to the precedence and vital significance of the reward idea in the Pauline eschatology."[3] I would go as far as to say that the frequency of Paul's mention of reward warrants calling this a near obsession. In 1 Corinthians 9:24–27, the apostle wrote:

> Do you not know that in a race all the runners run, but only one receives the prize? So run that you may obtain it. Every athlete exercises self-control in all things. They do it to receive a perishable wreath, but we an imperishable. So I do not run aimlessly; I do not box as one beating the air. But I discipline my body and keep it under control, lest after preaching to others I myself should be disqualified.

Corinth hosted the Isthmian Games, which were similar in importance to the Olympics. He used this metaphor to show how athletes trained and sacrificed with their hearts, minds, and bodies with the goal of winning the games. In the Isthmian Games, the victors received a crown. He says that these athletes labored for perishable crowns that had temporary reward. In gospel ministry, Paul makes similar sacrifices but for a much greater reward, a

---

3 Geerhardus Vos, *The Pauline Eschatology* (Grand Rapids, MI: Eerdmans, 1953), 273.

crown in heaven. Paul does not fear losing his salvation. He fears losing the reward of giving Christ a great offering and forfeiting the joy and pleasure that come with that. Again, it is not fear of punishment but fear of loss of an opportunity of reward.

The doctrine of rewards appears throughout the New Testament; it is not unique to Paul. Jesus himself exhorted his followers: "Do not lay up for yourselves treasures on earth, where moth and rust destroy and where thieves break in and steal, but lay up for yourselves treasures in heaven, where neither moth nor rust destroys and where thieves do not break in and steal" (Matt. 6:19–20). Jesus encouraged the pursuit of heavenly reward. Clearly such motivation is not selfish!

Jesus knew that setting our hearts on eternal treasure would purify the trajectory of our lives. He stated, "For where your treasure is, there your heart will be also" (6:21). When we walk with a vision of God in heaven and with desire to gain reward by pleasing him, such a posture can only sanctify a person.

Finally, Paul's missional motivation focused on serving the Lord by helping and investing in people. He wrote to the Philippians, "Therefore, my brothers, whom I love and long for, my joy and *crown*, stand firm thus in the Lord, my beloved" (Phil. 4:1). In 1 Thessalonians he also referred to his disciples as his *"crown* of boasting before our Lord Jesus at his coming" (1 Thess. 2:19). Paul equates his crown to the people with whom he had shared the gospel and discipled—their spiritual growth with his reward. Ralph Martin wrote that this notion contains the belief that "at the last day, the triumph of grace will be seen in the perseverance of the saints to the inexpressible joy of their spiritual mentors."[4]

---

4   Ralph P. Martin, *Philippians: An Introduction and Commentary*, vol. 11, Tyndale New Testament Commentaries (Downers Grove, IL: InterVarsity Press, 1987), 171–72.

The starting point of this investment in people involves evangelism. After discussing rewards at the judgment seat of Christ in 2 Corinthians 5, Paul identifies believers as "ambassadors for Christ" who make "his appeal" (2 Cor. 5:20). This appeal is the gospel, which brings those estranged from God into his heavenly kingdom. From the position of being in Christ in heaven, Paul implores believers to draw others into it through evangelism.

Can't you just see how refining, meaningful, and hopeful the heavenward life is with regard to missions and service? Living with the expectation of the coming of Christ moves us to live with an urgency that can spring us out of bed in the morning. It focuses our minds on the service of man in the service of Christ and provides godly motivation for work with eternal value.

Your Life Matters

Certain personality types may feel some level of pressure or anxiety as we talk about the doctrine of rewards. Scripture intends to convey to all believers through these two realities that every life in Christ has eternal significance and meaning.

We live in a world that celebrates greatness and celebrity, while overlooking and marginalizing mundane faithfulness. At times we hear this mantra in the Christian world: "Do great things for God! Make a huge impact!" That mantra is not inherently wrong, but what about the mom whose life involves endless days of changing diapers, treating clothes stains, making meals, and not sleeping? Or the home nurse who has sat with the same person with dementia nearly every day for five years, answering the same question sixty-five times per day?

In the self-help book *Fierce, Free, and Full of Fire*, Jen Hatmaker wrote, "Dear reader, YOU ONLY HAVE ONE LIFE TO LIVE. What if you die tomorrow having never given your dream a shot?"[5] Note that an eschatological notion—"You only have one life to live"—drives the author's battle cry. While pursuing dreams sounds inspiring to some, aspirations such as this are a luxury for affluent people in the western world. Let's keep in mind that about half of the world lives on less than $5.50 per day, or $2007 per year.[6] For the food-insecure father in sub-Saharan Africa, the poor farmer in Indochina, or the single mother in the slums of Kolkata, India, there is no concept of self-actualization and chasing dreams. The same is true for the vast majority of the billions of people in the world today or throughout human history. For most people, securing the next meal, living in safety, caring for their families, and enjoying some relationships maxes out life aspirations. Life is a struggle and is mundane at the best of times.

Even in the affluent, western world, very, very, very few people live spectacular lives. For just about everyone, life involves working a job, cleaning your home, caring for family, going to doctors appointments, paying bills, running errands, watching television, and some fun with friends here and there. For some people the most excellent form of self-actualization may involve cleaning out that junky closet, planting some flowers one weekend, or jogging two miles.

So where is the meaning for the regular person who is just struggling through life? This notion of eternal reward brings

---

5   Jen Hatmaker, *Fierce, Free, and Full of Fire: The Guide to Being Glorious You* (Nashville, TN: Thomas Nelson, 2020), 113.

6   Elizabeth Howton, "Nearly Half the World Lives on Less than $5.50 a Day," World Bank, October 17, 2018, https://www.worldbank.org/.

immense meaning to mundane, thankless service. Paul wrote, "He who plants and he who waters are one, and each will receive his wages according to his labor. For we are God's fellow workers. You are God's field, God's building" (1 Cor. 3:8–9). Neither the apparent impact nor the sexiness of the service matters in God's eternal economy. God values the work of the planter and waterer all the same. Service done unto the Lord with a worshipful heart is service done unto the Lord. Period. God rewards equally.

A seminary professor of mine had a child with significant special needs. His life consisted of working at the seminary and then taking over for his wife in caring for their child, which involved grueling work and supernatural patience. The two of them rarely if ever had a date night and never had a vacation. He told me that he had not slept through the night once in the thirty-plus years of his son's life. Don't you know that this father and mother's treasure in heaven will be every bit as great as that of Billy Graham's for the service they did for their child?

On a mission trip in North Carolina, my students had the privilege of serving a married couple named Lincoln and Lorraine. Lincoln had suffered a paralyzing spine injury at the very beginning of their marriage. When Lorraine walked down the aisle at her wedding, her dream likely did not entail nursing her immobile husband for the entirety of their marriage, until his death. Nevertheless, this was the mission field to which God called her. My students had the privilege of observing this saint demonstrate a truly spectacular life before their eyes as she served with joy, gratitude, and humility. Don't you know that Lorraine's reward in the kingdom of heaven will be every bit as immense as that of Mother Theresa's?

Living for treasure in heaven brings meaning to every mundane deed and prayer offered out of love for God that usually receive absolutely no recognition or accolade in this life. Washing dishes for your spouse, listening to your roommate, baking cookies for your neighbor, serving in the kitchen, extending kindness to people in the checkout line, and offering a prayer for a grieving friend—all of these mundane deeds, when done in the Spirit, glean eternal reward. The regular deeds of regular people on regular days possess so much eternal potential and meaning! The Lord sees, recognizes, and rewards all of them in heaven.

Furthermore, so many people labor for Christ and see so little fruit in this earthly life. This is the story of children's ministers, nursery workers, youth pastors, and, often times, parents. You plant seeds and plant seeds. You labor and labor. You try to build a foundation in young people based on the word and the gospel. You offer thousands and thousands of prayers. Then, you send these young people into the next stage of life, and you may never see them again. You have no idea what fruit the Holy Spirit may have borne in the lives of these young people. You have no idea if that seed you planted in the heart of a four-year-old at vacation Bible school came to fruition through the power of the Holy Spirit fifty years down the road. So much of ministry to young people involves a discipline of planting seeds, praying, trusting God, and anticipating reward at the judgment seat of Christ. God occasionally reveals glimmers of fruit here and now, but the vast majority of the fruit and impact comes in glory.

Paul declared, "Therefore, my beloved brothers, be steadfast, immovable, always abounding in the work of the Lord, knowing that in the Lord your labor is not in vain" (1 Cor. 15:58). Indeed, friends, nothing done unto the Lord will ever escape his eyes, go unrecognized or unrewarded. Your labor matters.

The Judgment Seat of Christ

All these matters related to the missional mindset in the heavenward life distill into one prevalent image in Paul: the judgment seat of Christ.

The judgment seat of Christ stands as one of the most confusing, hard-to-understand aspects of biblical eschatology. For many years I felt a sense of perplexity and fear when I read 2 Corinthians 5:10: "For we must all appear before the judgment seat of Christ, so that each one may receive what is due for what he has done in the body, whether good or evil." *Wait a minute. I thought I was saved from judgment and condemnation. I thought God judged Jesus on the cross for my sins. So will God evaluate me—both the good and the bad—in eternity? Will I have to pay for my sins after all? What happened to justification by grace through faith, and what about the cross?*

People have varying opinions regarding what 2 Corinthians 5:10 fully means. I want to offer a brief explanation of why the judgment seat is not something to avoid out of fear but instead to engage because of the hopeful and refining effect. The judgment seat of Christ has a valuable place in the life of the believer.

First, we need to define what exactly the judgment seat is. Believers do not go before Christ's seat upon entry into heaven, but at the second coming of Christ. As you can see, it does not make sense that eternal salvation would be at stake at this moment, because at that point most believers will have been with God in heaven for an extended period. Believers in heaven are not currently fretting about the judgment seat, nor will they. They live in and enjoy the perfect love of God.

Going before Christ here does involve an examination of the quality of our lives. We will not receive punishment for our sins here. When Paul refers to the evaluation of good and bad in 2 Corinthians 5:10, the bad refers more to missed opportunities and loss of reward. The Weymouth translation, in fact— a nineteenth-century common English translation—used the terms "good and worthless" in 5:10. What Paul has in mind more likely resembles what the 1662 Anglican Book of Common Prayer refers to as "things which we ought to have done" in its general confession of sin.

Given this sense of evaluation, should we be afraid? Tests and examinations inherently make one nervous, right? We can see that Paul approached the judgment seat with apparent expectation and hopefulness. He demonstrates no signs of fear or anxiety. (And I seriously doubt any of us will be sitting before the glory of Jesus prior to his second coming worrying about the judgment seat; that is an impossibility.) In this same paragraph Paul declares that he is of "good courage" and that he longs to be with Christ (2 Cor. 5:2–6). He views the judgment seat with joyful expectation.

The key to understanding the judgment seat comes in 2 Corinthians 5:9, where Paul writes, "So whether we are at home or away, we make it our aim *to please him.*" As Paul joyfully and realistically fantasizes about being with Christ in heaven, the affection that naturally stirs leads to a desire to please Jesus. Then a connective conjunction, "for," bridges 5:9 to 5:10, demonstrating that his affectionate longing to please Jesus leads his mind to the judgment seat of Christ. The image of the judgment seat does not evoke fear or anxiety but instead stirs up a warm passion to please and serve a person whom Paul loves.

I can identify with this sentiment from a personal story in my life. I once had a boss who hired me at a time when I was unhireable and unappealing as a candidate. I had resigned from another job for health reasons and could hardly work. I had no education or experience in the field of the business that he owned. The man offered me a job (in fact, a very good high-paying job) whenever I was ready, whether that was in three months or eighteen months. He encouraged me to take my time and to focus on getting back in good health. When I finally did work for this man doing sales, I worked hard, I tried to travel as cheaply as possible on trips, and I wanted to post huge numbers for him. I was not afraid that he would fire me or be disappointed with my performance. The man had been good to me, and he continued to bless me personally when I was with his company. My personal gratitude, love, and affection for him drove my efforts.

So it is with the judgment seat of Christ. There in the ultimate trajectory of our lives resides a man sitting on a throne before whom we will stand. However, this man is not aloof, angry, or displeased. No, on the judgment seat resides the Lamb of God, who took away each of our individual sins. There resides the good shepherd, who has walked beside us, gently tending to our lives with every step. There resides the Son of Man with all of his radiant and glorious beauty. And as you have this vision of that man on the judgment seat, know that when he sees you, he calls you by name and he smiles. With a vision such as this—a true and biblical vision—how can we do anything with our lives but offer them to him in love?

This is the moment for which Paul longed and the moment that motivated his tireless service and ministry for Jesus. This is the vision for you and for me. No fear or guilt compels us. Here is a vision of love that can motivate a rich, meaningful life. Every day of our lives constitutes one piece of the broader offering that we will lay before our gracious Lord at the judgment seat. Each prayer, each deed, each act, driven by the Holy Spirit, represents a part of a gift that we humbly lay before him as an expression of worship that ultimately communicates, "Thank you, I love you," to the Savior.

Before the judgment seat of Christ we receive rewards, the nature of which I do not know. Perhaps the reward is simply the opportunity to make the offering of our lives to the one who deserves an offering so great that we cannot comprehend.

Your Heavenward Journey

I am just a parent, like any parent, who wants to make his kids proud. No, I do not live for my kids' approval. At the same time, I want to live the kind of life that my children will view with respect and admiration.

The concept of making your kids proud changes quite a bit when one of your children lives in heaven. My little boy, Cam, does not care if I make buckets of money or drive a fancy car or gain lots of attention or achieve great success or win book awards. This child that I want to make proud is glorified and no longer sins. He has seen the face of Jesus and has far more wisdom, purity, and perspective than any sinner in the fallen earth today. Because Cam lives in heaven, he would view my life more like Christ would, in ways that I cannot imagine while in the flesh.

If I could theoretically consult him across the gap between heaven and earth about what would make him proud, he would tell me to drop all of my selfish, prideful, worldly pursuits and to focus on humble, faithful, purehearted service unto the Lord. He would tell me to share the gospel and disciple people. He would tell me to focus on the kingdom above all things.

If you have a loved one in heaven, these sentiments likely ring true for you as well. Regardless, a great way to calibrate ourselves is to think of our whole lives as an offering to God, as a gift that we will lay at the Lord's feet.

Conceiving of life in this way can send some people into a performance spiral. Before we think about offering our lives, we have to recall that Christ has already offered his to make us right with God by grace apart from works. God's pleasure dwells upon us irrespective of our good or bad deeds. God loves and relates to us based on the performance of Jesus in his life, death, and resurrection.

When we operate out of this love, which we first received from God, we then can live our lives in such a manner that, in the end, we can present a beautiful gift at the feet of Jesus in glory.

12

The Courage of Heavenward

No Fear in Death

IF YOU HAVE EVER sat ringside for a person's death, you will reso-
nate with this self-evident but true statement: death is the worst
thing in the world. Nothing in human experience can compare to
the horrors and misery of the dying process. If you've ever observed
a person shimmying through the death rattle and gasping for their
last breaths, you understand the accuracy of this sentiment.

If you've experienced a loss of any significance, the pain and
disorientation of a person dying tells you deep in your soul that
death is not "natural," as some people say. Death does not feel
right. That's because it's not. It is not in accord with God's har-
monious design for creation. Death is the deepest, most awful
manifestation of the fallout from original sin. Death stands as
God's chief enemy.

Given the ultimate terribleness of death, Christians too often
take for granted the absolute and supreme greatness of Christ's

victory over it. We take for granted far too often that Christ bestowed upon us the single greatest gift—everlasting life in heaven.

As horrific as death is and as inevitably guaranteed as it is for every single human being, so many people live with an alarming and, at times, delusional indifference toward it. They maintain a shocking level of ambiguity.

In the movie *Little Miss Sunshine*, a young girl, Olive, asks her father soon after her grandfather's death, "What's going to happen to Grandpa?" An awkward and chilling silence hovers over the car. Her father and mother have no answer. At all. Miles down the road, Olive asks her uncle Frank, "Do you think there's a heaven?" Her uncle's ambiguous reply: "That's hard to say, Olive. I don't think anyone really knows for sure." Meanwhile, her grandfather's corpse lies in the trunk of the car. (It's actually a hilarious part of the movie.) This is not theory. This is not a philosophical conversation in a college class or at a local coffee shop. There is the dead body of a cherished loved one six feet away.[1]

A similar moment of despair-filled ambiguity comes in the movie *My Sister's Keeper*, where a teenage girl, Kate, is dying from cancer. Kate and her sister, Anna, lie on a blanket in the sun and talk about the afterlife. Anna asks Kate if she's scared, and Kate answers no. Then Anna asks her dying sister where she thinks she will go. Kate responds ambiguously, "I don't know—but who knows?"[2]

As a person who is often around death, the ambiguity about the afterlife that I observe in these movie scenes terrifies me. As a person with stone-cold confidence that I will see my little boy

---

1   *Little Miss Sunshine*, directed by Valerie Faris and Jonathan Dayton (Century City, CA: Searchlight Pictures, 2006).

2   *My Sister's Keeper*, directed by Nick Cassavetes (Los Angeles, CA: Warner Brothers, 2006).

and my father and my grandparents and my friends again, another person's nebulous and amorphous conception of the afterlife makes me want to scream, "Wake up! How can you live like this?"

I have cited scenes from two movies, fictional people with no eternal answers for life after death. However, I have seen this horrifying eternal ambiguity in real life. I once attended a prayer and support meeting for a person dying from a severe form of cancer. The meeting included some Christians and some secular people. People went around the circle and offered support and encouragement. A woman in the group with the most sincere intentions offered this advice to the woman who had anywhere from six to twelve months to live: "When I have a hard season, I go take a vacation, and it just seems like the problems I left behind are not as great when I return. Maybe you can take a trip to gain some perspective."

Here in the face of certain death with the clock ticking, the best hope this woman had to offer involved a vacation. As my head swiveled back and forth between the friend and the woman facing death, a sinking feeling pulsated in my heart. *In the face of the worst thing in the world, taking a vacation is your best solution?*

In a 2008 *ER* episode entitled "Atonement," a former prison doctor who administered lethal injections to seventeen death-row inmates wrestles with his guilt for all the people he put to death. His career has ended, and he is now dying. In the scene, EMT workers wheel him into the emergency room, and he cries, "If I die, I am going to hell!" While the man expresses his guilt and fears over damnation, a "new-agey" hospital chaplain feeds him empty, "nothing burger" platitudes that provided zero clarity or comfort. In rage the man snapped at the chaplain:

I'm old. I need answers, and all your questions and uncertainty are just making things worse. I need someone who will look me in the eye and tell me how to find forgiveness because I am running out of time. I need a real chaplain who believes in a real God and a real hell.[3]

Here lies ground zero of human existence. Here resides The Question of life: What happens to me when I die?

From the Best Thing to the Worst Thing

Perhaps the greatest and most underrated fruit of the heavenward life is that Christ has delivered us from desperate ambiguity and given us eternal clarity. Even more, Christ has flipped death from the most dreaded thing in existence into the single greatest source of joyful anticipation for the believer in Christ.

Second Timothy is the last New Testament letter that Paul wrote. At this point, Paul knew he would soon die. The door had closed. In 2 Timothy 1 he encourages Timothy not to be ashamed of the gospel and to share faithfully in the sufferings of Christ. The basis of this exhortation resides in the clarity and confidence with which he approaches his end.

He remembers that God has saved him by grace and not by works, which is important. Our certainty of heaven emanates from the reality that God has forgiven all our sins through Christ's perfect work and made us perfectly acceptable for entrance into eternity. Our salvation hinges entirely on God's perfect works and not our imperfect efforts.

3   *ER*, episode 13, season 14, "Atonement," directed by Stephen Cragg, written by Michael Crighton, featuring Maura Tierney et al., aired January 17, 2008.

Believers throw around the word *saved* so frequently that we lose the depth and richness of its meanings. We forget exactly what the Lord has saved us from. God has delivered us from death and from eternal separation from him. He has solved the major problem any human being will ever face and answered the question, "What happens to me when I die?"

Paul speaks with a total confidence of his deliverance. He refers to Jesus as the one who has "abolished death and brought life and immortality to light through the gospel" (2 Tim. 1:10). The Greek word for "abolished" also translates as "unemployed" or "to put an end to." Jesus has put death out of business through his atoning blood.

I spent many, many years in school, including high school, college, graduate school, and then seminary. I hated exams, and heaven knows I took hundreds of them. Even though my own schooling and exam-taking are distant in the rearview mirror of my life, each December and May, when students from my church take tests, I take a deep sigh and say, "I am so, so, so glad that I'll never have to worry about exams ever again." So it is with death. Christ has put it in the rearview mirror of life for the believer in Christ. It's not something we have to worry about any longer.

Not only does Jesus solve the problem of death; he transforms something dreadful into a central source of joy and hope. A remarkable and unique aspect of Christian salvation involves the positive, celebratory way in which believers regard death. Jesus flips death from the worst thing ever to the best thing ever!

Listen to Paul's tone from his de facto death bed as he talks about the conclusion of his life:

> I am already being poured out as a drink offering, and the time of my departure has come. I have fought the good fight, I have finished the race, I have kept the faith. Henceforth there is laid up for me the crown of righteousness, which the Lord, the righteous judge, will award to me on that day, and not only to me but also to all who have loved his appearing. (2 Tim. 4:6–8)

Paul indicates that his death is imminent, and yet he expresses not a speck of fear. Not a hint of despair. Instead, Paul looks forward to his death, expecting that he will receive reward from the Lord.

When his life hung in the balance as he wrote Philippians, Paul declared, "For to me to live is Christ, and to die is gain. . . . My desire is to depart and be with Christ, for that is far better" (Phil. 1:21–23). When faced with the preference of life or death, the apostle considered death the "far better" option; he called it gain. He considered dying and going to Christ in heaven "far better" than remaining on earth.

A hospice nurse whom I know once had a conversation with a secular person whose husband was passing away. The wife expressed a sense of respectful jealousy toward the nurse, who is a believer. She told her that she envied the way that Christians viewed death with such positive anticipation and joyful triumph.

Christian writings throughout history bear witness to the hopefulness and positivity with which believers can view death. The first stanza of the American gospel song "Angel Band" demonstrates this positive tone:

> My latest sun is sinking fast,
> My race is nearly run;

My longest trials now are past,
My triumph has begun.
Oh, come, angel band
Come and around me stand;
Oh, bear me away on your snow white wings
To my eternal home.

The singer characterizes life as a "race" and as "trials," whereas his passage into death he refers to as "triumph."

St. Francis of Assisi described death in a similar way in the hymn "All Creatures of Our God and King." In the sixth stanza we sing:

And thou, most kind and gentle death,
waiting to hush our final breath,
alleluia, alleluia!
Thou leadest home the child of God,
as Christ before that way hath trod,
O sing ye, O sing ye, alleluia, alleluia, alleluia!

Death, kind and gentle? Yes, in the economy of the gospel. Death becomes an awaited mercy and relief because Christ has paved the path to heaven, and Christ will lead us to paradise.

Listening to the lyrics of these songs captures the hopeful expectations around death in Christ in such a manner that death becomes something for which we long. (Note that I am not talking about the process of dying, which can involve much misery, discomfort, and pain. The physical agony and the saying goodbye to loved ones is excruciating. I'm talking about our passage into eternity.)

I once watched a documentary series, *Limitless*, on National Geographic about intermittent fasting and its potential to prolong human life spans. Chris Hemsworth, the star of the *Thor* movie series, and a longevity physician fasted for four straight days in the episode "Fasting."[4] A part of the documentary involved explaining how not eating for extended periods of time can potentially help people live longer. The scientist demonstrated intense focus on extending life as many years as possible.

Yea, no thanks. I'm not interested.

I do think we all need to be good stewards of our bodies and of our lives. Within reasonable bounds, we should pursue healthy lifestyles through diet, exercise, and sleep, and avoid damaging patterns that can reduce our life span through negligence. I do not think smoking a bunch of cigarettes, drinking large quantities of alcohol, and eating terrible food constitutes good stewardship of our bodies. Following basic practices to promote good health represents Christian faithfulness.

Simultaneously, I want no part in this conversation of prolonging life. At a gym, a trainer once tried to sell me vitamins, and he talked constantly about extending my life span. I stopped him and said, "Pal, I'm not interested in staying around here any longer than necessary." I have no desire to live on this earth a second longer than what God has ordained for me. I'm not cutting out Diet Coke or ice cream, and I surely am not going to fast for four days in order to live here any longer than God intends (as if I have any control over that anyway). I want to be as faithful and fruitful as possible while I'm here and to enjoy the blessings

4 *Limitless*, episode 3, season 1, "Fasting," directed by Kit Lynch Robinson, featuring Peter Attia, et al., aired November 16, 2022.

of this life. However, I'm ready to get home. I'm ready to see my Savior, and I'm ready to see my son.

An elderly friend of mine who died in 2023 exhibited this eagerness for heaven as well as anyone I've ever seen. Five days before her death, I sent her a text to let her know that I was praying for her and that I appreciated her. In response she wrote, "Thank you so very much for your kind words, Cameron. I am sooo looking forward to going home to be with my Lord, something I've tried to prepare for all of my life. So glad that God is finally calling me home."

Yes, indeed. The worst thing in the world has become the chief thing we can anticipate and long for all through the wonderful work of Christ in the gospel.

Christian Swagger over Death

Modern technology and healthcare advances have seduced many (if not most) people into foolishly ignoring the realities of their mortality. In 2020 the United Nations estimated that the average life expectancy in the United States is seventy-nine years old.[5] In nations such as Japan, Italy, and Australia that number rises into the mid-eighties. In 1900 the life expectancy at birth in the United States was forty-seven years old.[6] As a result, many people live today thinking that salvation and eternity are matters that can be deferred, as they assume that they will live into their eighties.

Furthermore, modern people in developed countries are often shielded from death. Before modernity, most people died at home

---

5 "U.S. Life Expectancy 1950–2023," Macrotrends, accessed July 20, 2023, https://www.macrotrends.net/.

6 "Mortality in the United States: Past, Present, and Future," Wharton School, University of Pennsylvania, June 27, 2016, https://budgetmodel.wharton.upenn.edu/.

around their families. The family had to prepare and dispose of the corpse of the deceased. Today, many people die in hospitals. Families pay funeral companies to deal with the corpse. Funerals often have a closed casket. For both of these reasons most people quite honestly live assuming that they are not *actually* going to die.

This is not accurate. Life is fragile. I have observed the vulnerability of life in having four babies. With one of our pregnancies, my wife's amniotic fluid tanked such that her womb was nearly empty at thirty-five weeks. Without the benefit of sonogram technology and an early, induced delivery, the baby was at great risk of an umbilical cord issue that could have killed him. Another one of our children had respiratory syncytial virus (RSV) as a seven-week-old. His oxygen levels declined to the low-eighties. Without supplemental oxygen for five days he likely would not have survived. Of course, the premise of this book involves the sudden, unexplained death of my three-year-old son in his sleep. On that night there was a one in 625,000,000 chance that he would die in his sleep, and it happened.

When I was four, I swallowed a piece of hard candy while jumping around at my brother's basketball game. A person noticed me choking. The game was stopped. The Heimlich maneuver did not work. I began to turn purple. A nurse shoved her finger down my throat to extract the candy after several minutes of no oxygen. Were it not for the nurse's skill, I would have died.

All people need to live with an appropriate respect for the fragility of life. We need to treasure our days and make the most of the opportunities to serve the Lord and share the gospel. But there is one thing we absolutely do not need to do: be afraid. Quite the opposite. In fact, we need to possess an attitude of confidence and boldness in the face of death.

My favorite defensive back in football is Deion "Primetime" Sanders. Many consider Primetime one of the greatest all-around football players due to his status as perhaps the top cornerback and the top kick returner ever. After his playing days, Sanders then ventured into college football coaching, where he is known as "Coach Prime" and had instant success from the beginning of his career.

Sanders has an exuberant confidence that is magnetic. Many companies have sought him as an endorser, and recruits flock to him largely because of his positive swagger. This swagger conveys a belief that he will succeed every time and all the time. Primetime never talks trash, but his dominant play implicitly taunts opponents.

Jesus has defeated death so completely that a Christian can walk with swagger in the face of death with certain expectation of victory. Paul exhibits this swagger in the way that he literally taunts death in 1 Corinthians:

> "Death is swallowed up in victory."
> "O death, where is your victory?
>   O death, where is your sting?"

> The sting of death is sin, and the power of sin is the law. But thanks be to God, who gives us the victory through our Lord Jesus Christ. (1 Cor. 15:54–57)

It's as if Jesus has knocked death out cold in a boxing match and it cannot stand up. Paul hovers over death, taunting it, saying, "Get up! Come on, what's your problem? Get up!" Jesus has dominated death to such a complete degree that a believer can have this level of swagger that rides on Christ's undefeated record in his death and resurrection.

John Donne, in his poem "Death Be Not Proud," portrays this Christian swagger over death. In the poem he personifies death and speaks to it, opening with this condescending jeer:

> Death, be not proud, though some have called thee
> Mighty and dreadful, for thou art not so.

Donne takes the opportunity to set death straight and to remind it of its defeat, saying essentially, "Death, you may have been something at one time, but, now, you are a nobody. Have a nice day."

George Herbert expresses similar sentiments in his poem "Death":

> Death, thou wast once an uncouth hideous thing,
>> Nothing but bones,
>> The sad effect of sadder groans:
> Thy mouth was open, but thou couldst not sing.

> But since our Savior's death did put some blood
>> Into thy face,
>> Thou art grown fair and full of grace,
> Much in request, much sought for as a good.

Talk about spiritual trash talk! Death, Christ has thrown blood in your face. He has defeated you and insulted you in the process and made you into an impotent loser!

I encourage you to walk with this victorious sense of swagger before death. Celebrate Christ's triumph!

The day of my son's funeral I made a decision not to wear black, and I encouraged friends to do the same. I wore a light-colored suit. I refused to give death as much credit as to wear black. *No way.* My child had died but had instantly entered into the presence of Jesus in heaven. Christ had won the war on the cross two thousand years ago, and he won the battle on the day of my son's death. Cam's euphoria in heaven as a product of the gospel belittled death to its rightful place of failure and impotence. Christ's victory grants us this spiritual swagger before death.

Your Heavenward Journey

I do not look forward to the process of dying. I have seen enough people agonize through that process to know its misery. Simultaneously, when I know that my hour has come, I imagine that I will say, with happy tears and a smile, "At last, Cam, at last. This is what I've been waiting for since 2013." In reality, it's what I have been waiting for since the day I came to faith in Christ, to see Christ face-to-face and to be delivered from this painful life.

Remember often the eternal victory over death that Christ has given you. With all the problems you face in life, often recall that Jesus has solved the only ultimate problem that any of us truly face: he has secured our place in heaven forever.

Epilogue

Reunion

ON THE DAY AFTER CAM DIED, a pastor in his late sixties said, "You're going to see your son again, and it will be in the blink of an eye. Just you wait and see." I resented the remark in that moment. I felt such intense sorrow and missed my child so much that I heard these words as, "The next time you'll be happy will be when you die." But ten years later, I remember these words and agree. I'm going to see my son again. In relation to eternity, which I'll spend with him, it will be like the snap of a finger.

He won't be the only person I long to see and know. I'll see family members who have gone before me, like my father, and I'll know them in a way I never knew them in this life, as their glorified selves, perfectly as God designed them to be. There will be family members whom I never met, like my grandmother who died before I was born, and four siblings whom my mother miscarried.

There will be friends whom I wish there was more time to see in this life, like my believing friends from Wake Forest with whom

I shared such rich community. There will be plenty of time in eternity. There will be friends for whom, in the present, distance has grown, but we will be perfectly unified with Christ and without sin, having no need for boundaries. We will be able to have safe friendships with people of the opposite sex without having to worry about anyone getting the wrong idea or crossing any lines.

And there will be people whom I've always dreamed of meeting. I once got to hear Johnny Cash play one song (yes, only one song) at a music festival. I look forward to sitting down with him and being friends. I once stood ten feet from Bono in the inner ring of a U2 concert. It will be cool to shake his hands and have a conversation in the new heaven and new earth.

We will be able to stand before Jesus face-to-face and ask him questions and walk with him and actually see the smile on his face when we are in his presence. We can gaze up and enjoy the beauty of God without impediment.

We can fellowship with the apostles and the great figures of the Bible and church history. Won't it be something to know Martin Luther or Augustine?

These kinds of thoughts sound a little crazy, but it's all real and all true. When we get to heaven, there will be no limits of time, no hierarchy of people, no sin to separate us, no lack of resources, no hurries. We will have eternity in every sense of the word.

This kind of theological imagination helps us. It helps to engender hope, because it reminds us that everything that feels lost and limited as a product of sin, every way in which we feel short-changed by the fall, will all be regained. Jesus will renew all things. The Father will take back everything that belongs to him, including the many ways he has intended to bless his children.

And this truth gives me hope and comfort. It enables me to accept God's will in the short life of my son because I know that every experience and moment that feels forfeited in this life due to his death will be restored a millionfold in the world to come. And the losses of this life will feel like absolutely nothing—like a penny that rolled down a drain—compared to the life Cam and I will have together in God's eternal kingdom.

And it won't be long. At all.

Come, Lord Jesus.

Acknowledgments

I FEEL LIKE ANYTHING I accomplish always involves a large team of helpers and supporters. I would first like to thank my wife, Lauren, who is simply the best! She has been generous and supportive in allowing me to tell both our story and the story of our little boy. She lets me read every chapter to her, draft by draft, and offers great feedback and abundant encouragement. You're the best wife, Lauren!

Second, "Coach" Kathy Lawrence, my seventh-grade English teacher from 1992, is central and vital to my writing as my chief editor. One of the joys of my life has been going through every single chapter with Mrs. Lawrence. Coach, this is *our* project! Thanks a million, and God bless you!

Third, four men at Reformed Theological Seminary played a major role in this book, and I've thought often of their kindness and brilliance as I have written it. The late Kevin Collins and Dr. Nick Reid compassionately and kindly moved mountains to make seminary education possible for me with the challenges I faced following my son's death. Dr. Greg Lanier and Dr. Michael Allen gave me remarkable guidance and education to help me have a level of depth in Pauline theology to write this book. When I think of the completion of this book, I think of you with much gratitude and affection.

In any endeavor I have to thank my mom, who has always believed in me, particularly my overinflated aspirations.

To my children on earth, Knox, Hutch, and Mary Matthews, you are the best cheerleaders! Thanks for your patience as I've spent so many hours working on this book and for all of your love and support. I couldn't write this book without you. To Cam, God continues to use your life and testimony. What a gift—praise the Lord!

To the wonderful people at Crossway, particularly Dave, Todd, and Samuel, for giving me the opportunity and for nurturing me along the way.

Finally, many thanks to the people of the Advent who have been great encouragers and allowed me to teach on heaven so much in all of these years. I especially thank the many stars on the youth team and college interns who've endured hours of me obsessing over Pauline eschatology and union with Christ. Thanks to TPD and JT for being awesome initial readers, and to Charlotte "Chaschi" Getz and Anna "Team Mom" Harris for always having my back. Much love to our small group. To my hall of fame class of 2023 guys Bible study, for your prayers and support. To all of the people in the Rooted family: you put so much wind in my sail. A shout-out to the Bama Brethren and, as always, a shout-out to my boys, the Heavy Hitters.

Christ carries me through great friends. Thanks be to God.

General Index

Scripture Index